Words of Praise

"This book offers a compassionate and empowering path for anyone ready to stop trying to control the world around them and instead understand the world within. By reframing triggers as teachers and guiding readers inward, to their beliefs, their stories, and their connection to Source, it steers us toward deeper self-awareness and our own true power. A soulful companion for anyone ready to stop managing the outer world and start transforming the inner one."

Christine Lang, Energy Healer, Spirit Channel and Author of Ask Your Spirit- Receiving Life-Changing Wisdom from Your Elevated Intelligence, www.christinelang.org

***

"From the moment I met Rev. Rachel, I knew we were speaking the same language. The language of the soul remembering itself.

Recover Your Soul is not a 'how-to' book; it is a lived journey of awakening, courage, and divine remembrance. Through her story, Rachel offers a sacred mirror for anyone who has ever lost themselves in addiction, control, or codependency and longed to come home to their true self.

We walk parallel paths, each guided by Spirit to discover that we were never broken, only disconnected from our wholeness. Her story is honest, raw, and profoundly spiritual, a memoir that opens the heart and reminds us that healing isn't about fixing what is wrong. It is about remembering who we have always been."

Ester Nicholson, Spiritual Teacher and Author of Soul Recovery – 12 Keys to Healing Dependence www.esternicholson.com

"Reverend Rachel's spiritual memoir offers deep insights and relatable stories that will undoubtedly lead many readers to a happier and more fulfilling future. Stories of journeys and epic quests are always exciting, and her deep dive into exploring her soul's path is particularly engaging. I am very pleased to know that my Akashic Records teachings have been supportive of her ministry."

Dr. Linda Howe, Teacher and Author, Linda Howe
Center for Akashic Studies www.lindahowe.com

***

"Reading Rev. Rachel's deeply vulnerable and honest account of her journey toward wholeness was truly inspirational. Her reflections resonated with me on a personal level. I saw myself in so many of her thoughts and emotions. Her insights invited me to approach my own story with greater curiosity, compassion, and hope."

Julie Dunbar, Author of _Exploring World History through Geography: From the Cradle of Civilization to a Globalized World_

***

"As a member of Al-Anon, I found Rachel's podcast on my many walks during the pandemic. It was divine timing to find her message when I needed it most. I have remained a loyal participant of her Recover Your Soul community. So often, the time limit of her podcasts left me wanting to learn more about her journey. Her book beautifully provides the "more" I was seeking. Her honesty, humility, and vulnerability make her story relatable. Her transformation and healing give the reader hope. In a time of distractions, noise, breaking-news overload, despair, and frustration, Rachel's story is a light in the darkness, a peaceful message that we are being held by something greater and that we are always loved and never alone. Namaste."

Diane M, Al-Anon and Recover Your Soul Community Member

A Spiritual Journey of Healing from Addiction, Codependency, and People-Pleasing

REV RACHEL HARRISON

In collaboration with Mattie Murrey

Recover Your Soul:
A Spiritual Journey of Healing from Addiction, Codependency, and People-Pleasing

By Rachel Harrison and Mattie Murrey

ISBN: 978-1-968960-05-6 (Paperback)
ISBN: 978-1-968960-06-3 (Ebook)

Library of Congress Control Number: 2026904147
Cover Design by Andrew Magee

Printed in the United States of America

Upword Publishing
Denver, CO

upwordpublishing.com
First Edition

"Rachel's gift of words and wisdom through her coaching and workshops has changed my life. This book is a treasured resource for accessing the guidance that I can count on when needed. So grateful."

Stacey Mendez, Artist *www.staceymendez.art and Recover Your Soul Community Member*

Table of Contents

Dedication

This book is dedicated to my inner child, who has remembered her light again.

This book is dedicated to the sacred soul within each of us.
The part that arrives open, clear, and innocent, and then journeys through the wild adventure of being human. Along the way, gathering wounds that shape our stories, create our beliefs, and form the patterns we live by, yet beneath it all we are not broken. Our true essence remains whole.

This book is dedicated to remembering.
To a gentle returning to our brilliant light.
To the quiet wisdom of the Higher Self that has walked with us through every moment, waiting for us to listen.
To the awakening that shows us that even the hardest seasons have purpose in the pain, guiding us back toward truth, compassion, and love.

And it is dedicated to every tender soul who is longing to let go of the pain and fear.
May you remember your wholeness.
May you feel the presence that has never left you.
May you know, with clarity and grace, that healing is possible and that you can Recover Your Soul.

Acknowledgements

It is the steps we walk together that give the journey meaning. My story can only be shared because of the beautiful souls who have been by my side.

To my husband, Rich, and to my sons, Alex and Bodhi: thank you for being the heart of my life and for allowing me to share so many parts of our story in these pages and on the podcast, trusting that our experiences might bring light to someone else's path. We have called ourselves *Team Harrison* for decades, and it continues to be a sacred reminder that we are in this wild ride of life together, no matter what. Thank you for loving me through every stage of my healing and for showing up with open hearts as we all learn and grow. I am forever grateful for the depth of love we share.

To my parents: thank you for living lives rooted in creativity, joy, and authenticity. You said "I love you" easily and genuinely, and that gentleness taught me to speak love freely in all my relationships. Thank you for seeing me, encouraging me, and giving me the space to become exactly who I am. To my mother, thank you for opening the door to the spiritual world with such curiosity and wisdom, allowing me to find my own path. To my father, thank you for nurturing my creativity, encouraging me to write my own songs, and teaching me the value of being unique.

To my friends and spiritual sisters: although I grew up without siblings, life has blessed me with beautiful souls who have filled that space in the most meaningful ways. Some were with me only for a short season, offering exactly what I needed in those tender moments before our paths diverged. Others have stood beside me for decades, becoming the siblings of my heart, witnessing my life, loving me through every chapter, and offering a steadfast presence that has shaped who I am.

And to the sacred sisters who have come into my life during this era of healing and awakening, the ones with whom I can speak freely about Spirit, energy, intuition, and the magic of awakening, thank you for seeing my soul and shining so brightly with me. Your love, your honesty, and your willingness to walk this path together have been a profound gift.

To Mattie: what a blessing it has been to walk this journey with you. You encouraged me to begin the only way I knew how, by recording my stories as I had done on the podcast, and you helped me shape those beginnings into a manuscript. You offered tools, guidance, and unwavering support through every rewrite and transformation. You gave me permission to write the book that felt true to me and came behind me to smooth the edges so that these pages could fully reflect the Recover Your Soul journey I have walked. Your friendship, wisdom, and steady belief in me have meant everything, and I could not have done this without you and your team at My Own Ghostwriter!

To the rooms of AA and Al-Anon: thank you for teaching me how to be honest, how to listen, and how to surrender. Your wisdom, humor, and kindness saved my life. Every story shared, every hug, every reminder to "keep coming back" created a foundation of healing that I still stand on today.

To the spiritual teachings that shaped my awakening: from Unity and Buddhism to metaphysics, sacred texts, and the many teachers whose voices have guided me, thank you. I have been blessed with access to so much wisdom and Truth, and each teaching arrived exactly when I needed it. You helped me see with new eyes, shift my perception, and remember my wholeness as a soul in human form.

To the listeners and community of the Recover Your Soul Podcast, and to every client and event participant: thank you for trusting me with your healing journey and for letting me know how my journey has touched your own. Your messages, your courage, and your willingness to recover your soul alongside me have meant more to me than I can ever express. I feel your love, and I hope you feel mine too.

To Britton and Alyssa at Upword Publishing: thank you for guiding me through this process with such skill, patience, and kindness. Your steady support helped me bring this book into the world with confidence and clarity. And to Solara, my AI assistant, thank you for helping me organize years of podcast transcripts, journal entries, and ideas and for reflecting my voice back to me with such gentleness and insight. This support has been a true gift on my creative journey.

And to Spirit, to my Higher Self, and to the guides who have whispered to me throughout my life: thank you for never leaving my side. Thank you for the quiet encouragement that finally broke through when I was ready to let go of the pain. I can see now that I was never alone and that the loving, compassionate guidance I felt was always there. Learning to listen to my soul has been the greatest gift of this journey, a reminder that only love is real.

May this book be a whisper from your Higher Self.
May it offer comfort, clarity, and hope.
May it remind every reader that they are loved and whole and that their soul knows the way.

With profound gratitude and love,
Rachel

Foreword

My name is Rich, proud husband and life partner to Rachel. I'm here to introduce a book about her journey of physical, spiritual, and emotional recovery - a spiritual path that transformed not just her life but our entire family.

She and I came together, as many do, around the lures of sexuality and partying. We connected immediately and enjoyed every adventure, especially when we were packing along the proper alcoholic provisions. Many of you know the feeling, I'm sure...when you fall in love *and* you find your perfect party buddy!

As for me, I began the sex, drugs, and rock & roll lifestyle very early. I was blessed to be born and raised in the heart of Los Angeles with all of its glitz and privileges, but it all seemed to come at a cost in the end. I was 14 years old in 1980 and already chasing that crazy train of popular parties and the next best dopamine rush. Weed was already getting smoked, the alcohol was abundant, and my brother gave me my first line of cocaine at age 16.

The thing is that I was very functional and on a good track. I was a good student and a budding artist, and I was raised in the country club life by my highly respected father, a professional golfer and revered PGA instructor. Believe me, I knew how to be a gentleman. Did this serve to camouflage what an insatiable party boy I was? Well... it didn't have to. Everyone within and around my family was doing the exact same thing! It was what we all did, family and friends alike, and it was normal - for us. Actually, it was the catalyst to every good time, and it was the reward at the end of every great day.

And then a couple of years into marriage, Rachel suddenly says, "We should have kids now so that we won't get too old to be great parents!" Regardless of whether we were ready or not, we made two beautiful boys together, Alex and Bodhi, and gave it all we had. I was launched into the role of financial provider and got quite serious about working my ass off.

Rachel and I were building a beautiful life together with awesome people all around us and celebrating daily with lots and lots of drinking.

I loved my family fiercely, worked extremely hard, and tried to do everything right. This approach, combined with my desire for big adventures, resulted in a profound "intensity" that was experienced by the rest of the family. As Rachel was settling into our home and raising the kids, I was building up my skill sets and being an excellent provider....so I thought. It turns out that Rachel was feeling abandoned and alone with our young children, especially while I poured myself into building the family cabin on her mother's 35-acre mountain property.

The project was cathartic for me at the time. I had designed the cabin and was building it right out of the solid granite mountainside with my own two hands. It was so special to me, which was the reason it was also blinding me to Rachel's emotional needs and her increasing discontent. It also took my alcoholism to another level.

Rachel and I made our first attempt at sobriety through a combined moment of clarity. We wanted to be even more present with our young children, and what a smart thing to do! Our intentions, strong as they were, only began a long and fragmented journey into the unknown and unhealed pieces of ourselves and our complex codependent relationship. And so, we tried and failed many times, in many ways, over the next ten years or so.

Our marriage nearly failed, and I experienced the darkest days of my life during the year we separated in 2014. These were extremely trying times, and both our boys were descending into drug abuses and addictions of their own.

As a deflection from our own issues, or simply the inability to release from our pain bodies, we constantly argued and obsessed over the boys. Our family was cut in half, with Bodhi and I in one home and Rachel and Alex in the other. Nevertheless, my love for Rachel remained intense, and I held onto the possibility of reuniting the family one day.

What happened next is Rachel's story of recovery. This book describes a journey that was deeply her own. Even though we traveled this road together, we each had our own experience of what was happening. She took her final drinks on an adventure to Thailand with her mother and made a commitment to sobriety that continues to this day. More critical was the deep dive she took at turning within, descending into the inner work of healing that was to come.

Rachel's love for our family is deeper than the ocean, and she is one who puts everyone else's needs before her own. Her dedicated work has helped her to deepen this love while also releasing her need to control and be the "fixer."

As I was one of the things she wanted to change and fix, I have witnessed and benefitted from how fantastically liberating and healing this has been for both of us. As for myself, I cannot claim eight solid years of sobriety, but I have been on my own path of recovery that has changed me to the core. Being alongside Rachel's deep studies into recovering one's soul through practice and spiritual consciousness, she has shared a deep blessing and a priceless gift.

I can claim to be living a sober and spiritual lifestyle that is like a phoenix emerging from the fog of a former alcoholic life. Once you break free of the control and addictions to Recover Your Soul, you can see and feel that it becomes a whole new experience of living...clearer, cleaner, and far more loving.

As you read this book, you may be feeling hopeful and connected, or you may be in a season of deep pain. I believe that you will see both and find it all relatable through Rachel's journey to recovery. I'm here to testify that it is possible.

There is no light without darkness, and no matter how deep the despair can be, change is possible. Healing is possible! It's not perfection by any means, but rather a greater honesty and presence to the present moment.

My hope is that countless others, through Rachel's story, will feel inspired to find their own willingness for honest self-reflection and deep healing.

I am proud and deeply grateful for what Rachel has created through her journey and this book. Recover Your Soul is her memoir and the story of the light that led her out of darkness into deep spiritual connection and personal transformation. It's also about her family being rebuilt from the inside out and the love that flourishes when two people are brave enough to heal together.

Welcome to Rachel's journey. May it inspire your own.
With love and gratitude,
Richard Harrison

Before you Begin

Welcome. I'm so grateful you are here.

As a hippy child born in 1970, I was raised in a home steeped in Tibetan Buddhist philosophy, where conversations about compassion, karma, and the soul's evolution were part of everyday life. Those early teachings gave me my first understanding of suffering and the possibility of awakening, long before I ever had a name for it.

Later, Unity became my spiritual home for more than two decades, teaching me the power of prayer, metaphysics, and the Divine presence within all things. And when I finally followed the inner nudge to step fully into ministry, I studied and was ordained through the International Metaphysical Ministry- a nondenominational organization rooted in universal spiritual principles.

These traditions all share a deep belief in our innate wholeness and in the soul's capacity to awaken. These are the threads that have shaped me. And even with all of these teachings, I still had to walk through every moment of my own life, including the heartbreak, the patterns, and the pain, to arrive where I am now. Nothing was skipped. Every step and story mattered and had purpose in its lessons.

This book is both a story and a companion. It is a reflection of my own healing and awakening told through the lens of the **Recover Your Soul™ 9-Step Process of Healing and Awakening,** a process I created during my own journey.

These steps didn't arrive all at once. They came to me slowly, through lived experience, through the 12-Step rooms that saved my life, through grief and surrender, and through prayer, journaling, and the quiet moments when Spirit whispered what I most needed to hear.

I didn't set out to create a process. I set out to save my own life. What became the Recover Your Soul Process grew out of my journals, my tears, my sobriety, and those soft, insistent nudges from my Higher Self saying, *"It's time to heal. Recover your soul."*

Over time, the steps evolved, first as a shortened spiritual interpretation of AA and Al-Anon, and later as something deeper and broader as I worked with clients and continued to awaken myself. In 2024, the steps clarified themselves into the 9-step process you'll meet in these pages.

This process is living and breathing. I am still walking it, still learning from it, still being shaped by it. And my hope is that it will become a light for you too, wherever you find yourself on your journey.

You'll notice as you read that the stories don't unfold in a strict timeline. They move around to reflect the healing within the steps. This is because healing is not linear. Each section has its own awareness and is, at the same time, part of the whole. Our souls reveal things in their own timing. The early chapters carry more of the rawness, pain, struggle, and the patterns that once held me captive in drinking, codependency, and control addiction. These stories matter. They show the depths from which awakening becomes possible.

As the book moves forward, the lens shifts. The stories become less about external drama and more about the inner landscape and how my perception changed, how my soul came forward, how the light slowly returned, and how I remembered my wholeness and came to live fully from my Higher Self.

A central part of my healing was recognizing that we are eternal souls, walking human stories. I believe we come here with soul contracts, with lessons and relationships chosen for our growth. You don't have to share that belief to find value in this work. What matters is that you remain open to the possibility that your life, even the hardest parts, has meaning.

Throughout this book, you'll find QR codes that link to the book's resource page offering podcast episodes related to each chapter's themes. Over the past several years, I've shared my awakening in real time on the **Recover Your Soul Podcast** and the **Recover Your Soul Bonus**

Podcast, with over 550 episodes to date, each one forming a living archive of this journey: raw, imperfect, and honest.

These QR codes are simply invitations, not assignments. They point you toward stories and conversations that expand on what you'll read here that is far more than could ever fit into these pages. When you scan them, you'll be taken to a landing page where you can easily explore the episodes and resources that call to you, at your own pace.

You will also find my songs woven throughout these pages, songs I wrote through heartbreak, surrender, and moments of grace. Music has always been one of the ways my soul speaks.

This book is an invitation to begin your journey to **Recover Your Soul.** To know you are not alone, and to maybe see your story through my story and choose a spiritual path to healing and awakening. The Recover Your Soul Process is not something to "finish." It is a way of living, a way of remembering who you truly are beneath the patterns, the pain, and the stories.

And as this book shares the path I walked, my memoir, I am working on the next book, which will be a more detailed guide of how to use the process in depth as a full guide to follow this powerful and transformative spiritual path of healing and awakening. At the end of each chapter you will find a starting place and simple guide, but know that there is more coming, and that with the podcasts and all the resources I offer, your journey has just begun.

Take what resonates. Leave what doesn't. Trust that your Higher Power knows why you are here at this moment and that you are exactly where you are supposed to be on your journey.

You are not alone.

Your soul remembers the way.

All you have to do is listen.

With love and gratitude,

Rev. Rachel

Remembering Who You Are

Awakening begins the moment you choose yourself. - RH

There's a voice within you that knows and remembers your wholeness.

No matter how lost you feel, how broken your life seems, or how impossible the pain appears, there's still a small voice that whispers the truth your soul has always known: You are not here to be small. You are not here to drown in suffering. You are here to remember who you truly are and to shine that light into the world.

I know this voice exists because I almost lost it completely. For more than 20 years of my life, I was convinced that everyone else held the keys to my happiness. If my husband would just stop drinking, if my children would make better choices, if my family would be the way I needed them to be, then I could finally be OK.

I was attempting to control what felt unmanageable. I became a masterful fixer, a professional people-pleaser and codependent, and eventually, an unhealthy alcoholic, all while desperately trying to save everyone around me from their own pain.

What I discovered, when I finally surrendered to what I now call the Recover Your Soul™ Process, was that the very thing I had spent years running from, my own inner awakening, was the only path to the freedom, peace, and joy I'd been seeking all along.

This Is Our Story

Being someone who doesn't generally draw attention to myself, it feels vulnerable to share this story with you. But I want to share it not because it's my story, but because it's our story, humankind's story. It's a story of healing, of awakening, of remembering, and of recovering the soul that gets buried under years of trying to be what others need us to be.

This narrative is the incredible hero's journey we all walk as souls. It is about letting go of the control, complexity, and pain we often find ourselves trapped in, and rediscovering who we truly are.

In sharing my journey, I hope to give you permission and encouragement to value every memory, every experience, and everything you have walked through as part of *recovering your soul*. It is a sacred process that transforms wounds into wisdom and pain into purpose. **I know this transformation is possible because I forgot who I was for a long, long time. And then I remembered.**

The Moment Everything Changed

Eight years ago, if you had told me that I would be living in a transformed marriage with a husband who has become my best friend, watching my sons thrive as independent young men following their passions, writing this book as a sober, ordained metaphysical minister, and hosting a podcast that reaches thousands of people seeking their own spiritual awakening, I wouldn't have believed you.

I wouldn't have believed you because eight years ago, I was drinking myself to death, convinced that my family was irreparably broken, that I was a failure as a mother and wife, and that there was no way out of the pain that had become my constant companion. I had tried getting sober before and failed. I had tried therapy, tried controlling everyone around me, and tried everything except the one thing that would actually save my life: choosing myself.

The moment everything changed did not come in a dramatic revelation but in a simple recognition during a car ride home from the airport. After three weeks in Thailand—my last-ditch attempt to detox before what I secretly believed might be my final surrender to alcoholism—I was thrust back into the familiar chaos of my family's dysfunction. As my husband launched into his usual complaints about our struggling son, I felt that old tightness in my chest, that familiar urge to fix and manage and control and numb the pain.

But something was different. For just a moment, I saw our situation with startling clarity. I saw a family trapped in patterns of pain, each of us using our own coping mechanisms to survive, and I saw that I had been just as caught in the dysfunction as everyone else. More importantly, I saw that the only person I had any real power to change was myself.

In that moment of grace, I made a decision that would change not only my life but also the lives of my entire family: I was going to get sober for myself. I was going to stop trying to save everyone else and finally choose to save myself.

What is Recover Your Soul?

Recovering Your Soul is more than standard recovery or sobriety, though that was certainly part of my journey. Recover Your Soul is a spiritual path to remembering and reclaiming your authentic self—the self that exists beyond the roles you play, the expectations you try to meet, and the pain you've been carrying. It is a spiritual path to a happy and healthy life; it is a process of healing and awakening

It's about releasing your attachment to controlling others and outcomes and instead learning to trust in something greater than yourself while taking full responsibility for your healing and happiness. It's about understanding that you are not broken and never have been and that there is a wholeness within you ready to be awakened.

The 9-Step Recover Your Soul Process to Healing and Awakening isn't just a program I created; it's the path I lived, stumbled through, and ultimately found my freedom on. It is how I recovered my soul. Each step represents a crucial shift in perception, a release of old patterns, and a deeper connection to the truth of who you are.

And these are the 9 steps that have been created in my journey, and I will be walking through them in the following chapters:

Recover Your Soul™ A 9-Step Process to Healing and Awakening

1. Ready for Awakening

Recognize Suffering: Become aware that your dissatisfaction and suffering are rooted in your current perceptions, beliefs, patterns, and stories. *Acknowledge the Need for Change:* Understand that this awareness is the first step toward awakening and transformation.

2. Release Control

Identify Attachments: Recognize that your pain and suffering come from attachment to control and the illusion of power over external circumstances. *Embrace Powerlessness:* Accept that you are powerless over everything outside yourself, and that true strength and peace come from within.

3. Discover Unhealthy Patterns, Beliefs, and Stories

Examine Patterns, Beliefs, and Stories: Identify and acknowledge the unhealthy patterns, beliefs, and stories; often formed in childhood and shaped by family, culture, and conditioning that have influenced your life and behavior. *Recognize Their Impact:* Understand how these unconscious patterns have created suffering and shaped your perception of self, others, and the world.

4. Open to Co-Creating with a Higher Power

Explore What Higher Power Is for You: Define and explore your personal relationship with Source, Spirit, God, Higher Consciousness, or Light. *Connect with Your Higher Power:* Begin to co-create your life with the Higher Power of your understanding, choosing compassion, authenticity, and trust.

5. Release Old Patterns That No Longer Serve You

Cultivate Awareness and Insight: Use your growing awareness to gain insight into your old patterns and beliefs, and to recognize what you have learned from them. *Practice Compassion and Forgiveness:* Release these patterns through awareness, compassion, and forgiveness both toward yourself and others so you can make space for healing, peace, and new ways of being.

6. Embrace New Beliefs and Rewrite Your Story

Update Your Mindset: Step into new beliefs and patterns that align with your Higher Self and expanded perception. *Recognize Your Gifts:* Acknowledge your unique gifts, assets, and strengths as you rewrite your personal story from a foundation of truth and love.

7. Align with a New Perception

Shift Your Perception: Align with a new, healthier perception of yourself and the world around you. *Choose Your Reality:* Consciously shape your experience by aligning thought, word, and action with your awakened perception and Higher Self.

8. Deepen Your Spiritual Practice

Commit to Presence: Develop regular spiritual practices that keep you grounded in the present and connected to your Higher Self and the Higher Power of your understanding. *Live in Alignment:* Continue to release old stories and embody the principles of Recover Your Soul as a daily way of being.

9. Shine Your Light

Live Authentically: Let go of control and judgment, embodying your True Self and allowing life to unfold with grace and acceptance. *Be a Beacon of Love:* Allow your presence and peace to inspire others, becoming a light for awakening and transformation in the world.

The Courage to Remember

What you'll read in these pages is my story. My journey through addiction, codependency, and near-divorce was messy, painful, and often heartbreaking. There were moments when I genuinely believed I would be better off dead. There were years when I couldn't see past my own pain and resentment. There were times when choosing myself felt like the most selfish thing I could possibly do and I felt as if I were abandoning my family.

But here's what I learned: Choosing yourself isn't selfish. It's sacred. When you heal your own wounds, when you remember your own wholeness, when you step into your authentic power, you don't just transform your own life, you become a catalyst for healing in every relationship you touch.

The transformation in my family didn't happen because I finally succeeded in controlling them. It happened because I stopped trying to control them and instead became someone worthy of the love and respect I had been craving. **When I released my death grip on everyone else's journey, they were finally free to find their own paths to healing, and I was free to find mine.**

An Invitation to Freedom

This book invites you to remember who you are beneath the pain, patterns, and stories that have kept you small. It's an invitation to step off the emotional battlefield and into the peace that is your true nature. It's an invitation to trust that your healing is not only possible but inevitable when you align with the spiritual principles that govern transformation.

You don't have to wait until you hit a rock bottom. You don't have to lose everything before you choose to save yourself. The moment you're ready—and you'll know when that moment comes—the door to Recover Your Soul swings wide open.

Your soul is calling you home to yourself. All you have to do is listen.

Together, we can do the work that will Recover Your Soul.
— Rev. Rachel Harrison

Book Resources

Learn more about the podcast and explore the community

Book resource library

CHAPTER 1:
My Story

*"The day came when the risk to remain tight in a bud
was more painful than the risk it took to blossom."*
— Anaïs Nin

We all have a life story that needs to be told. It is our unique walk on the hero's path. These experiences are what make us who we are and form the foundation of our soul's desire to experience all that there is to experience in this lifetime, at times to a depth that we may not fully understand. Our pain and challenges in life are often what offer the most growth and opportunity for awakening.

The call is to tell your story as your truth, derived from your own thoughts and viewed through the lens of your experience. Your story does not reflect how anyone else saw it or felt it, as it is uniquely your own, much like your fingerprint. Uniquely yours.

When we can gently witness our life, both the light and the shadow, and see how beautiful and essential it is, we can begin to embrace the fullness and wholeness of ourselves.

We can accept and see that there are no wrong turns in our lives, only opportunities for experience and an invitation to learn from all that we feel.

As I wrote and rewrote this book, along with Mattie at my side, I was trying to convey the duality of who we are in our walk of life. First, we have a Higher Self, which is our eternal soul that never loses sight of our wholeness and unlimited nature. Then there is the other part, which I call the small self, the one that feels all the humanness and constructs the pain stories trying to make sense of the complex experiences we have.

Our Higher Self and human self. Both these parts combine to complete our whole selves, and how we see and perceive our life is a reflection of who we are within. The light shining from our Higher Self, and the shadow expressed through our small and human self. Together, they form our whole self. When we can finally understand the value of our shadow and the value of our story as we see and experience it, our transformation can begin.

So I will share my story with you. The first part is filled with the pain, my pain. Our pain matters and is here to show us and teach us in ways that can be hard to understand when we are walking through it. My family members hold other stories, and each of them has their own view and feelings about our shared experiences. I do not claim that this is what "happened," only that this is how it felt for me.

And even in my darkest hour, when I was drowning in my suffering and pain, I felt my Higher Self there loving me and guiding me to find the path, to heal, and to remember who I am and who I am here to be. **May this be a reminder that all of you and your stories matter and that wherever you are on your journey, your Higher Self is leading the way.**

My Story as I Felt It

In 1994, when I was 24 years old, I stood at the edge of a lake surrounded by a small group of family friends, gazing at my prince. Having ridden in on a white horse, guided by my father and stepfather, I made vows to a man I thought was perfect. We had a love that was deep and incredibly blissful. We looked into each other's eyes and made promises of love and dedication that were pure and honest.

I know that on my wedding day, I couldn't possibly have imagined the complexity and difficulty that was to come.

My husband, Rich, and I had been connected partly through a lifestyle of partying. When I met him for the first time on my 22nd birthday, which, oddly enough, I have on videotape because I had just bought a video camera as a present to myself, we were both trying to have the most fun we could possibly have.

When we eventually reconnected later that year, he was my prince charming: blonde hair, blue eyes, with a vitality in life beyond anything I had ever witnessed before. He was handsome, charismatic, talented, and kind, and... he liked to party like I did.

I didn't understand at the time that this was the seed of pain being planted in our lives.

I Wanted a Fairytale

We all have this idea that there's going to be a beautiful happily-ever-after when we fall in love. Even if we've experienced hardship during our upbringing, we believe that somehow it will be different for us. We want the fairytale, the unrealistic fantasy we saw on TV or read in books. We don't fully understand the complexity of life, which inevitably includes pain and challenges as part of the journey.

Looking back now, having gone through everything I've been through and having worked deeply and intensely on a spiritual path that has provided incredible transformation, I can see that everything I walked through had a purpose.

This was my soul's journey of self-discovery. This was my path to recover my soul. However, as we experience pain in real time, it can be hard to see its purpose, as our discernment is often clouded by our suffering.

I had bought a home before we got married, and once we were engaged and married, we lived together in a small house in Louisville, Colorado, where I dreamed of a beautiful family and an easy life. We both wanted a family eventually.

One day while we were out driving, I was having a conversation with some close friends who were a little older than me about why they were waiting to have children. I realized that I didn't want to wait and that I was being called to have a child right away. When I shared this with Rich, he was a little apprehensive. He wanted more time with just me before we brought a child into the picture, but he was willing to do whatever I asked of him. We were still in the idealized bubble of being madly in love and creating our life as newlyweds.

We were fortunate that, as soon as we began trying, we became pregnant with our first son, Alex, who was born in 1996, just four years after we started dating. However, in hindsight, our first child was born before my husband was really ready to be a father.

Everything seemed perfect in that first pregnancy. Rich was incredibly present, attending every doctor's appointment and taking care of me in a beautiful, kind, and conscientious manner. He was stepping up as a husband and provider. Although he had studied to be an architect, he discovered that he found it far more appealing to work outside with his hands in the dirt. So he became a stonemason and builder, determined to support his family and fuel his creative drive.

With incredible intent and kindness, we birthed the beginning of our family together.

The First Warning Sign

During that pregnancy, I had a business making flower arrangements, and one of my commitments was with a therapist. This blossomed into an opportunity to trade flower arrangements for therapy appointments, not that anything was wrong in particular. Rich and I had realized that our communication with each other could use work, and we felt therapy was a good idea that could head off potential problems.

During one appointment with our therapist, she looked us in the eyes and said, "You know, I think you may have a foundational issue in your relationship, and it may be around drinking and the possibility of alcoholism."

We left that particular therapy session thinking her insights were crazy.

Looking back now, I see that we were in denial, reluctant to face the truth.

I was not drinking heavily at that time in my life. It was easy for me not to drink when I was pregnant and nursing. I was absolutely enthralled with being a new mom and loved the idea of our growing family, so I fully stepped into the roles of wife and mother.

We had not initially planned on having more than one child, but it's no surprise that we decided to have another child. Two and a half years after Alex was born, we had Bodhi.

Blending of Spiritual Beliefs

One of the things I am grateful for in my life is my spiritual path, and I appreciate that even when I was not aware or listening to my Higher Self, Rich remained interested in and supportive of my journey. I was raised in New Mexico by parents who began following Tibetan Buddhism when I was a baby, during the time it was being introduced into hippy culture.

When Rich and I started dating, he was attending a large megachurch and going to Bible study with some people his age. His openness and curiosity about my beliefs made me feel safe and curious about what he believed. When we had Alex, we both wanted to bring our spirituality together and searched for churches that would be open to both of our belief systems where we could raise our son.

After 'church shopping' for a few months, we found our home in Unity, a metaphysically based Christian church that studied what they called 'New Thought,' a combination of both Eastern and Christian philosophies with a foundation on the mystic teachings, and was open to a wide variety of beliefs. It was an early seed to a foundational part of our life that would hold us in both our happiest and darkest times but was a constant that provided love and structure to our lives.

When the Dream Started Cracking

My journal entry from November 20, 1996:

> *A mother for over two months... Now a new definition of self:*
> *Rachel, wife, mother, daughter, friend. The problem is that,*
> *for me, I usually come last. I'm searching for a way to balance*
> *all those things.*

During my pregnancy with Bodhi, my mom and stepfather purchased a 35-acre piece of land two hours north of where we lived in Colorado. My parents worked with Rich, who designed a beautiful, small cabin. The dream was that it would be the beginning of a larger compound of homes on this acreage for our family.

This was ideal for Rich, as it allowed him to utilize his skills and creative energy. He could put his architecture degree into practice by building a house with his own hands for his family. It was a challenging project to take on.

There was no power at the site, so he lived off-grid, sleeping in a tent, and everything ran on a generator. He was excited to fulfill a long-held dream that would provide for his family in many ways.

So he went to fulfill that dream.

This was not, however, a dream for me. I felt that he had left me alone, and for almost three years he only came home on weekends. This was when I had a small toddler at home and was pregnant with our second child. After Bodhi was born, I was on my own, feeling very alone, and I cared for our children.

This is when I felt my marriage beginning to crack.

One way Rich coped with the grind and kept his passion alive was by drinking and drinking heavily. For him, and for the crew alongside him in those harsh conditions, alcohol became both their reward and their release.

It was evident we were living two separate lives. He was on an adventure, and I was nurturing my children. We were not having a sha-red experience in the same way we had when we were both partying together and had fun as our focus.

I felt very isolated and abandoned and did not know how to manage or even feel those feelings.

My journal entry from December 17, 1998:

> *I feel like I must drag him to help. He feels like I'm not giving him credit for the help he's giving.... I want him so much, and then when he's here, I feel like I'm just disappointed.*

My poem from November 17th, 1999:

Feeling isolated
Isolated and alone
Alone. Surrounded by sound
Sound of crying, laughing
Laughing with my boys
Boys, fill me with joy, frustration
frustration. For being without Rich
Rich gone
Gone. Changing without me
Me, changing without him
Him trying to complete his dream
Dream of a simple life together
Together sharing our thoughts
Thoughts and feelings
Feeling isolated

The Birth of My Control Addiction

I didn't recognize it then, but I see it clearly now: my addiction to control was born out of my suffering. It came from the constant urge to make things different, from dissatisfaction with the life I was living, from my blindness to what was working, and from my fixation only on what wasn't.

On our fifth anniversary, I stood on the hillside next to the cabin Rich was building with my 6-month-old baby in a backpack and my toddler holding my hand. As I reread my vows to my husband, I knew that my fantasy was beginning to crumble. I was questioning my life and marriage. I was already lost.

I felt that my perfect life, my perfect marriage, and my perfect family were already broken.

My discontent while Rich was working on this project simmered into a low-grade fire within me. It was always smoldering, even though

I didn't fully comprehend it, a constant feeling of resentment that left me feeling unsettled, upset, and never truly happy.

It undermined my ability to be present, even in moments when life was good and I should have felt happy.

That quiet flame of dissatisfaction kept me from settling into the life we had. The resentment fueled a restless determination to make things different, to fix what I believed was broken. I didn't recognize it as control at the time. I only knew I was fiercely determined to get our family and marriage back to the vision I had carried in my heart.

Our therapist's reflection on drinking, which I had once brushed aside, began to surface in unexpected ways. One of the ways I tried to reconnect with Rich was by drinking with him again after I finished nursing Bodhi, both as an attempt to bridge the gap between us and as a way to numb the feelings that were building inside me.

What began as a fun dinner with a round of margaritas often spiraled into bickering and fighting about anything and everything. The kids, disturbed by our erratic behavior, acted out, and the night usually ended with all of us angry or in tears. I was quick to notice Rich's mood swings and how they weighed on me and the boys but was far slower to recognize my own.

What I did know was that I rarely liked who Rich became when he drank.

The Foundation

But the truth is, my addiction to control didn't begin in my marriage. The seeds were planted much earlier, in the complicated relationship I had with my father after my parents' divorce.

When I was in fifth and sixth grade, I would take the Greyhound bus by myself for an hour to visit my dad in Santa Fe. Once or twice a month, I made that journey – a young girl navigating bus stations and highways just to have a few precious days with her father.

My dad had a lot of different girlfriends during those years after my parents divorced.

I learned early to shapeshift myself, to mold and adapt to fit into these sometimes uncomfortable situations. I became whoever I needed to be just to have those few days with him. I studied each woman, trying to understand what would make things easier and what would help me belong in whatever temporary family structure was forming around us.

I didn't know it then, but I was already learning the tools of people-pleasing and control.

When I was 13, my dad met the woman who would become his second wife. I initially believed she would be merely one of his numerous girlfriends, fleeting and similar to the others. But that was not the case. It was soon clear that this was different.

She had a son the same age as me.

Suddenly, we were pushed into a family system that I was not comfortable with. I didn't have the understanding at the time to express what I was feeling. I had no language for the confusion, the displacement, and the loss I was experiencing. I only knew how to be good, to adapt, and to shapeshift again.

My dad's girlfriend had created rules about how my dad and I could interact because she was uncomfortable with how affectionate we were with each other. In a moment, I felt I had lost my dad on every level. Suddenly, the effortless warmth we shared became inappropriate, requiring regulation and control from someone else.

And yet I was stuck with an obligation to be where I did not want to be.

The Trip That Changed Everything

Early in their relationship, the four of us drove cross-country together—from New Mexico to Texas to visit my dad's family and eventually to the East Coast to see where his girlfriend was from.

It was a difficult trip for everyone. Her son and I were both completely confused with this new relationship we were being forced into. Neither of us had chosen this family. Neither of us knew how to navigate it.

There was a lot of stress on that trip because they had very little money, and it was clear to us that it was causing issues between them.

At the very end of the trip, in Cape Cod, I asked for some money to get something to eat. What seemed like a simple request to a hungry teenager ended with a huge fight between my dad and his girlfriend.

I'm not sure what was actually said in that argument. But what I heard, what I internalized in that moment, was that it was not safe to ask for what I wanted or needed. Not even for food.

I instantly created a belief and built a protective wall around my heart, and I made a decision right then and there: I would not take anything from them so that I would not be a burden.

I felt completely out of control of my life, of my family, of who I was becoming.

I could control this—at least that's what I told myself. When everything else felt unpredictable and unstable, shrinking my needs down to nothing felt like the one place where I still had power.

I flew home from that trip with a deep sadness and a validation that I was not enough somehow. That my needs were too much. That asking was dangerous

The Eating Disorder

This marked the beginning of a two-year struggle with an eating disorder. I restricted my eating at their house in my determination to not eat their food, to not take from them, and to not be the problem.

It felt good to be in control.

And so this restriction followed me into my life living with my mom. The pattern I had created to protect myself at my dad's house became the pattern everywhere. I was getting attention from boys at school for being thinner, which only reinforced the behavior.

Along with having some protection at my dad's house, my high school years included an unhealthy way of caring for myself. Or more accurately, not caring for myself at all.

The cycle was broken when I looked at the scale one day and it read 111 pounds. At 5'8", something shifted. My Higher Self came online and shook me out of the trance I had been in.

I could see that I was harming myself in my attempt to punish someone else for hurting me.

I could see that I deserved more.

The truth was my dad and stepmother had never even noticed that I rarely ate at their house. They had no idea what I was doing or why. And I realized I did not want to harm myself anymore.

However, this was the foundation of a pattern of being obsessed with my weight that would last my whole life.

I would struggle with my value outside of being pretty or desirable before and during my marriage. At times, I found myself using weight as a form of control, such as gaining weight as a way to push Rich away from me when I was feeling unloved by him in our darker years.

The pattern of control I learned as a teenager of using restriction and self-harm to manage what felt unmanageable would follow me into my adult life.

I didn't recognize it then, but I see it clearly now: My addiction to control was born out of my suffering. It came from the constant urge to make things different, from dissatisfaction with the life I was living, from my blindness to what was working, and my fixation only on what wasn't.

The Parenting Battleground

My journal entry from June 5, 2001:

> *Rich doesn't see me. Or maybe I don't let him see me. I've built*
> *walls so high that even I can't remember who I am inside them.*

From the very start, it was clear that we each had very different parenting styles. Neither one of us had ideal modeling from our own parents. We both had come from divorced homes and families that dealt with addiction issues. We both had childhood foundations that didn't resemble the family we wanted, and we lacked the communication skills and role models to guide us.

So we were struggling to find our way, trying the best we could at the time, but it often didn't work.

I wanted to raise my children in an environment in which they felt only unconditional love and enjoyed a freer, more gentle style of discipline. Rich also wanted to lead with love, but he had very different ideas around rules and behavioral expectations.

Without realizing it, I was repeating the only pattern I knew—parenting as a single parent, just as my mother had. I didn't like or understand Rich's parenting style and often disagreed with how he interacted with the boys, disagreeing with his words, tone, and techniques. I didn't even agree with some of his values. Instead of being understanding or asking questions, I battled him and tried to fix and change his way of parenting. I wanted to control him.

I discounted and undermined what he was doing and saying. I focused on what I didn't like instead of having the ability to see, allow, and accept him for who he was, even if I didn't like it.

So we began a long and painful emotional battle, and I learned to pick up my tools of pain, grievance, control, and withdrawal.

The Beautiful Life I Couldn't See

When I look back at pictures and photo albums, they're filled with beautiful memories and snapshots of joy and laughter, all moments that seem like nothing but good times.

Rich was always the one to take the kids out, always coming up with activities to keep them busy and on the move. He had grown up skateboarding and surfing in Southern California, so it was natural that, practically from the time they were babies, our kids were propped between his legs on snowboards and skateboards as he pushed off, their tiny hands clutching his while the rush of wind hit their faces. It was his world, and he wanted to share it with them.

Our youngest took to it like he'd been born riding. By the time he was 2, he was already out at the snowboard and skateboard parks, tiny helmet wobbling, doing little tricks, and riding down the street all by himself. It terrified me and thrilled me at the same time.

Alex could ride, too, but his gifts showed up differently. From the very beginning, he was a brilliant artist. That was his natural talent. He would draw for hours, whole universes spilling out of his imagination. He built elaborate Lego castles and creatures and then turned them into stories with his toys and his brother, narrating scenes and characters with an intensity that pulled you in if you happened to be listening. That was Alex's magic, the way he created worlds inside the ordinary, turning simple moments into places where wonder lived and where we all felt a little more alive.

On so many levels, we really did have a beautiful life, but I couldn't see it, couldn't let myself feel it fully. I had shut parts of myself down just to protect my heart, and in that shutting down, I became overly focused on what wasn't working instead of what was.

I had grown up in a family in which conflict didn't exist, at least not openly. My parents never fought in front of me. My mother never raised her voice. So from a very early age, I learned to be a "good little girl," keeping the peace that felt both safe and necessary.

The problem was that I never learned how to handle conflict at all. When it showed up later in life, it felt dangerous, like the floor might fall out from under me. I didn't know you could disagree, argue, and even fight and still be OK afterward. To me, the only option seemed to be avoiding conflict at all costs.

Whenever there was conflict, I had no idea what to do with it. I didn't know how to hold it, how to stay with it, how to move through it. My only strategy was to shut down. And in that shutting down, a desperate desire to control grew. If I could just make it all OK, if I could make everybody and everything OK, then maybe I could be OK too.

Any fighting became incredibly difficult for me. Trying to keep everyone from fighting or being upset consumed my entire being. I felt that it was my job to avoid every conflict and, if I couldn't do that, then to fix any conflict.

I now realize that one of my unconscious core beliefs was that it was my responsibility to ensure that everything remained smooth and that there should never be discord, conflict, or a lack of harmony. Nobody should be fighting. No one should be in trouble. Life should be perfectly peaceful, all the time.

I didn't realize then how unrealistic that was, or how deeply I had taken on the burden of believing it was mine to fix.

The First Attempt at Sobriety

My journal entry from April 3, 2005:

> *Still waiting for the answer, I suppose. Maybe there isn't one. And being dissatisfied or uprooted emotionally is just the way it is. We are all more disconnected than ever, and maybe we can't really get past the cycle we continue to follow without some major changes.*
>
> *Sobriety is the first answer, and yet I feel like it will never happen. Not for real. I want to drink to get past my hurt from my separation and emotional distance. He drinks to relax and to have fun, to get away from his stress. I feel isolated and alone when I'm in my own home.*

In 2009, when my mother-in-law died, Rich and I found ourselves thinking back to the therapist who, years earlier, had warned us that alcohol was a problem. Denial was no longer an option. It was clear now that drinking had become a problem in our marriage and in our family.

The death of Rich's mother was unexpected, as she was young, only in her early 70s. We believed one of the reasons she passed was the lifestyle she had lived, one that included a lot of drinking. It had taken a toll on her body and may have contributed to the health issues and complications that led to her death.

Her death was a wake-up call for us. Not long after she passed, we made the decision together to try sobriety. Our boys were 10 and 13, old enough to notice, old enough to be shaped by our choices. We wanted to give them something different and to model better patterns, to show them healthier ways of living. Rich and I had been struggling so much with each other, but beneath it all, we still wanted the same thing: to be a healthier, happier family and to find our way back to being a couple again.

So in March of 2009, we walked hand-in-hand into the Alcoholics Anonymous meeting room on a Friday night. It was with such relief, and I felt that I was finally going to get my husband to be sober.

I didn't believe I was attending AA because I was an alcoholic. Yes, I drank, sometimes a lot, but that wasn't why I went. I went to sober up my husband. If he got sober, then we could finally be better. If he got fixed, everything would be fixed. That had been my prayer ever since he started drinking so much more heavily back when he built the cabin.

I went to that first AA meeting willing to work the steps, but I never really did Step One, which is the only step they say you have to do with your whole heart and soul. I never fully admitted that I was powerless over alcohol (or your addiction).

I told myself I just liked to drink. Deep down, I didn't believe I was powerless, and I didn't believe I was an alcoholic.

What I wanted was for my husband to stop drinking. That was it. I would have done anything to get him to stop.

For that first year, we went to meetings together, mostly side by side. It became one of the few ways we knew how to connect. And for a while, it worked. We began to experience real, positive changes in our lives. It gave us a pause, a kind of respite from the chaos and dysfunction. Things felt a little smoother, and for a time we touched something closer to true joy and connection.

I worked the 12 Steps with a sponsor. I did everything she asked of me and followed the program and its suggestions closely. Rich, initially, also had a sponsor and began working through the first few steps, but he never really connected with any of his sponsors. Within a year, he had stopped going to meetings altogether, maintaining his sobriety on his own.

I was determined to fix our family, so I kept going to my AA meetings and even tried a couple of Al-Anon meetings after Rich had stopped showing up. But I never truly committed myself to the Al-Anon program. My focus wasn't on hearing its message. It was on keeping Rich from drinking again.

At that time, I believed sobriety was the answer to everything. If he didn't drink, then maybe I could escape the mood swings and the intensity that made me so uncomfortable. I even gave him an ultimatum: "If you drink, I'll leave." And it worked. He wasn't drinking.

But without a solid path of recovery, without Rich's old solution of alcohol, the intensity remained, and our lives began sliding back into unmanageability. Since I wasn't the one with the drinking problem, I slowly stopped going to both programs. That left us with nothing but our old patterns of his anger and my control.

When the Boys Started Struggling

It seemed to only make sense that our oldest son, Alex, began to have problems at school. With our family issues at home and his highly sensitive nature, he was just responding to feelings he did not understand. He had been a different kind of learner from the start. When I look back now, one of my greatest regrets is that I was in denial here as well.

I was so focused on myself and my pain that I didn't see what he needed and how he would be best served with his learning style. I kept trying to fit him into a mold, the "perfect family" where, if everybody would just do the "right thing", then we would all be OK.

Both boys had been diagnosed with ADHD in elementary school, but we didn't grasp what that really meant. We couldn't. We were too caught up in our own addictions, in our own ways of seeing things, in our control, and in our overwhelm.

Now I see that this is the human journey: the complexity and challenge of life. Nobody gets to bypass the stickiness of it. As parents, there's an added layer of anguish when your children begin to grow into independent beings, carrying their own emotions and their own pain.

There came a time when I could no longer ease my children's pain with something simple like a cookie, a nap, or the safety of my arms. Their hurts grew bigger than what I could soothe away. They began watching me more closely, taking in who I was, not just what I said.

And without even knowing it, they started carrying forward the beliefs, stories, and patterns I had lived out in front of them. I saw pieces of myself reflected back in them, for better and for worse.

It was both humbling and heartbreaking. They were learning what it meant to love, to be loved, and to survive. They became a reflection of what I showed them: a mirror of the life unfolding around them, as well as of me and their dad.

Rich and I were still caught in our own struggles with our addictions, our broken communication, and our unfinished growth as human beings. That system was shaping our children just as much as it was consuming us.

By the time Alex had finished elementary school and moved on to middle school, he was really struggling. He was being severely bullied, and when he reacted, he got in trouble for the way he handled it. The school focused more on punishment than awareness, so instead of support, Alex was labeled as a problem child at school and even within our family.

Everything in our lives felt like a battlefield, and now it was constant. Every conversation, every day. Tension. Upset. Control. Rich and I fought endlessly about the kids. We both wanted a solution, but our views on how to fix our child and our family were completely different.

Bodhi began to play the role of peacekeeper in our house. Even with his own struggles, he learned to lie straight to our faces, telling us exactly what he knew we wanted to hear. It was his way of keeping the peace, of not rocking a boat that already felt like it was sinking. His playing the role of the golden child became how he tried to keep us all happy.

And apples don't fall far from the tree. By middle school, both boys had discovered marijuana as a way to escape the unrest in our home. Soon we were living with the familiar stories of the lies and broken promises, sneaking out, and choices we could already see would only lead to more trouble.

Things were really beginning to fall apart.

Dry Drunks

Although we were sober from drinking, we were not emotionally sober. We were not spiritually sober. We were what is called "dry drunks." We no longer had alcohol as the solution in our lives, but we hadn't embraced the solution that AA offers, that deep inner healing and the peace that comes from a spiritual awakening.

The 12th Step of AA begins with, "Having had a spiritual awakening as the result of these steps." Rich had not worked the steps, and although I had gone through them, I had never fully surrendered to the process or come close to a spiritual awakening.

What strikes me, looking back, is how our stories were never just one thing. The photo albums don't lie. There really were moments of joy and light, even when so much else was unraveling. Alongside the struggle, there were little reprieves, flashes of love, the kind of moments a camera could catch.

And when I look back now, I see how important those times were, the ones where we would shine through, where who we really were, our authentic Higher Selves and the family we longed to be rose to the surface.

Even though there was underlying disappointment and despair, there was so much that was holding the knowing that we, the four of us, four beautiful souls, loved each other, cared about each other, and wanted the best for each other. It was those moments when our souls reminded us, nudging us to remember not to get lost in the pain and to recall the love and feel the joy that was also there. Even in what felt like the darkest of times.

The Breaking Point

My journal entry from March 3, 2012:

What's my part? How am I feeling? I feel frustrated and numb. I've learned not to feel at moments like this. I've learned to shut down. Why is that? How can I support Rich and his feelings, but let my own desires help him get past his resentment? Not push him into anger.

I don't feel like I can continue to listen to him wanting everyone else to be different, to change, to mold to his ideal. That's been my trigger button for years. But here I am, wanting him to change! I want to hear his feelings, just not his resentments about how they're wrong, wrong, wrong. I'm trying to think and see if I ask for people to change, and I'm hoping that I don't do that.

I try to allow each person to sit in their own skin and have a deep understanding that we each have our own path. My deep sadness is the awareness that Rich and I just don't connect on a deep level. He doesn't feel heard by me, ever, and I'm not sure how to let him be.

Alex's 16th birthday in the summer of 2012 became a breaking point for our family. I was pouring myself into work, into music, leading a band at church, and writing songs, while Rich and I grew more and more distant. I could only see the parts of him I didn't like, and he felt that rejection deeply. Without alcohol to numb us anymore, we were both raw and defensive.

When Alex's aunt gave him a video game console for his birthday, it went against Rich's house rules and sparked an explosion. By then, I had become completely enmeshed with Alex's emotions, stepping between father and son instead of supporting their relationship. Rich wanted to raise a strong, capable young man, but all I could see was him being too hard on Alex.

That video game console became a symbol of all of our unmet needs, all the pain we couldn't name or handle.

At church one Sunday, when all the summer commitments were finally over, there had been a particularly good talk from Reverend Scott. I reached over to touch Rich's hand during the service. He pushed my hand away.

I recoiled instantly, and my old defense mechanism snapped into place like armor around my heart. The pain was overwhelming, and I was exhausted from the rollercoaster.

Separation

We decided to go for a walk after church. In the field behind our house, we had the same fight we'd been having over and over for what seemed like years. Same argument, same two people, same outcome. The only thing that was different was the setting.

What were we going to do about Alex? How could we fix this broken child? If we could just fix him, then maybe our family would be fixed. Rich was convinced Alex was the problem. I was convinced Rich was the problem. And so we battled.

I had hit a breaking point. I looked him in the eyes and said, "I can't do this anymore. I need a break." I packed a few bags and left for my mom's house, which was thankfully just a couple of miles away.

It felt surreal to finally do what I had been writing about in my journals for years. All that dissatisfaction and unhappiness, all those therapy sessions filled with blame and wishing he was different. And now here I was, actually packed up and gone.

I felt numb, like I was floating in a space I didn't understand. My mind went back to that day we stood by the lake and promised our love to each other. What happened to us? How did we get so lost? Where did it all go?

It wasn't meant to be permanent, just a break. I took Alex with me to my mother's house, and Bodhi stayed with Rich.

My journal entry for September 14, 2012:

> *I'm in a space where I'm shut down and want to run, run, run.
> I feel like the differences and the difficulties are just so present.
> I want to be joyous and simple. I'm not. We are not. It's not
> just these times, it's us. I'm so confused and I wish I could see it
> more clearly. I want us to be a family that loves each other, not
> only because we are blood, but because we really enjoy the time
> we spend together. I want us to laugh and for us not to be so
> heavy. It's so heavy. And so I ran.*

The Point of No Return

Over the years, we had gone to various counselors, including our minister, and after I left, we found a new coach from our church to help us work on our relationship. Those sessions felt different. They were the first honest and real work we had ever done in counseling, because this coach had an approach unlike any we had experienced previously.

I wanted to try, I wanted to open my heart, but there had been so much pain for so long that I struggled to see any real chance for healing. Still, we kept showing up week after week, telling the truth, possibly for the first time.

About two months into our coaching, Rich and I were on the phone talking when he suddenly stopped mid-conversation. He said, "Listen, if you already know what direction this is going, I don't want to be dragged along. If you already know where you want to go with this, you can tell me now."

In that moment, a door opened. A crossroads. I could feel all the years of confusion and pain rising up, and I remembered my dad telling me how he hadn't walked through the open door when it was presented to him in his second marriage. He said he spent many more years in unhappiness because of it. And here I was, staring at my own open door. A choice must be made.

So I gave Rich my answer. "OK. I actually don't want to be in this marriage. I want to be divorced." I walked through the door and chose a new path.

Rich was devastated. Angry. Hurt. He made a heavy plea for me not to walk through that door. He reminded me of the day we stood on the edge of the lake, making promises to each other. Marriage was supposed to be a commitment for a lifetime. He asked me to work on it, to give him more time to work on himself.

But I had made my decision.

Our parents were divorced on both sides. His parents divorced with anger and hatred. My parents divorced with love. I had grown up with the belief that you have different relationships for different phases of your life, for different chapters of your evolution.

Maybe that was true for us. Maybe the season of our relationship was over, and it was time to move on. I felt like I couldn't be my authentic self anymore. There was too much evidence that we weren't aligned, that even though we still had an underlying love, our lifestyles, our values, and the way we saw life just weren't the same. I wanted something else. I wanted a different life.

But I was scared, really, really scared, for Alex. I didn't like his and Rich's reactions to each other. I didn't like their relationship. I didn't like how our family felt. I didn't want this family, not the way it was. It didn't feel good to me. And leaving felt like the right and only choice, and I thought it would solve our family's problems.

My journal entry for November 25, 2012; The Next Day:

> *The thoughts are so confusing and have had so many layers to them. It's almost impossible to write them down and explain them. But what I can say is that the hours of conversation Rich and I have had yesterday and especially today have been honest, kind, connected, and real.*
>
> *I've not been sharing what was really going on in my head with him for such a long time, and I have a deep regret that*

I have not felt that I could be completely open. But now with nothing to lose, we are both being completely honest, honest about our deep love for each other, as well as our feelings of being stuck and dissatisfied over the years.

My heart is completely breaking as I walk away from this.... We are both scared to death to make the next move, to walk forward in our lives without each other. But I know that this is the right thing for me. I hope Rich can take this and decipher who he is and really have a chance to take life by the horns and go for it. I'm open to Spirit to show me my next step.

With this final break, we both went back to drinking. Rich no longer had the ultimatum hanging over his head, and I had, in fact, left. I was still clinging to the belief that I wasn't an alcoholic and had no reason not to take the edge off, to have a little fun. I turned again to the relief I had always found in the bottle, a temporary solution to my heartache and to the discomfort of living with things I wished were very different.

A Second Chance

We told the boys after Thanksgiving, in a therapist's office, after many difficult conversations, that we were getting divorced. Although they had lived through years of upset and dysfunction from both drinking and not drinking alcoholic parents, this was not what they wanted. I felt the brokenness of my family, and I felt responsible for their pain.

Alex fell even farther into a world that was growing dark and dangerous. Bodhi stepped deeper into the role of the golden child and peacemaker on the surface, but underneath he was cracking too, buckling under the stress of trying to hold us all together.

We started a new, separate life. Alex and I lived at my mother's house, and Rich and Bodhi stayed at our home across town. Christmas that year was strange and tense, with Rich and I both trying to hold it together for the boys. We took turns driving them into town to catch the bus to the local snowboarding hill and attempted to coparent.

Rich stopped drinking, hoping to show me that he wanted to be better and that there was still a chance for us. He softened in many ways, broken completely by our separation, yet not giving up hope and trying to be who he thought I wanted or needed him to be.

I poured myself into my job, where I felt needed and valuable. At the same time, I found a new freedom away from my marriage, the kind many feel after separation. Every weekend I was out with friends, going to bars, listening to live music, and drinking, often until I was drunk. And even though there were still so many painful and difficult things happening at home with Alex, I slipped back into one of my greatest defense mechanisms: denial.

After a few months of true separation, Rich and I went out for dinner together. I sat across the table from him, almost disconnected from the conversation. He was talking again about why we should try, and I was certain it was not what I wanted.

Then he said, "It doesn't seem fair that you are making a unilateral choice for three other people who want a different outcome." His words hit me like a bullet to the heart. In that instant, I saw that I would not be able to spend a lifetime carrying the burden of this choice.

Rich had spent the last two months making promises and implementing changes, and the boys had made their wishes clear. They didn't want our family to break apart. I realized I had to give it another chance.

In that moment, I wasn't sure if it was a chance to survive or a chance to fail. But I knew I had to step back in and let it unfold however it would. If we healed and grew stronger, that would be amazing. If it all crashed and burned, at least I would know that I had tried.

So I gave Rich the answer he had been looking for since the day I walked out. "I will give it another try."

My journal entry for February 22, 2013:

I feel myself justifying this. I'm convincing myself and others that it's going to be different, but in my heart, I don't believe it. If that is what I believe to be true, then why am I willing to go back to it? First, Rich loves me deeply and that feeling of admiration feels good. Second, I don't want to live my life alone. Third, I want to believe in change, and I know that there are dark times. The kids really make it hard at this point. Lastly, it's all I know.

Moving Back and the Descent into Darkness

My journal entry for June 28, 2013; the Day Before Moving Back:

I move back to Chestnut Street tomorrow, 9 months and 15 days from September 14th, 2012. I'll move back on June 29, 2013. I'm both happy to be moving back to Chestnut and also nervous. I know Rich loves me and has a desire to grow and be more in his heart and connected, but I still worry that we are just too different and may not be able to fit....

The effort that went into our dating period of only a few months already is gone and I want and need to find peace in the reality of the Harrisons' life at Chestnut.... The boys want structure, and we all need to learn how to do that together with gentleness, boundaries, and healthy communication. I don't want to have to be solo and do it all alone again. I want to be open, tender, kind, and vulnerable.

Alex had completely fallen apart. He was skipping school, using drugs, and was angry and depressed. We were lost. We had been lost for so long, desperately trying to figure out how to help him, how to save him.

I believe Spirit stepped in and guided us toward a local residential treatment facility. This wasn't just another addiction program. Alex's struggles went deeper than substance abuse. This place took a holistic approach, helping kids discover who they truly are beyond their pain and destructive patterns.

Through the generosity of friends and family, along with our small savings, Alex was admitted when he was 16 and a half. I pinned all my hope on this program, believing it might finally fix and save my son and my family.

I moved back home with Rich and Bodhi while Alex was in treatment. To reconnect, Rich and I turned again to our old friend, the one that had brought us together in the first place: alcohol. The rush of endorphins, the euphoria, the checking out, the laughter—it was all there waiting for us.

While our son was in rehab, we still believed he was the problem. If he could get well, get fixed, then we'd all be better.

Alex had done significant work during those five months and was better, but he returned to a home that was exactly the same. The same dysfunction, the same perspectives, and the same belief that Alex needed to do all the work for our family to heal. Except now his parents were drinking.

Looking back, I understand that alcoholism and addiction are family diseases. Dysfunction is a family disease. No one was at fault. We were all just wounded. I know now that no one's broken. We're just human beings trying to recover our souls, though that's not how I felt then. I believed that if we could fix the broken ones (and of course, that wasn't me), everything would be OK.

This child, just shy of 17, walked back into our unchanged home. And what do you think happened? He went right back to his old patterns, his defense mechanisms, his addiction, and his solution. He and Rich picked up where they had left off in their fighting. Everything slid back to how it was before, and I became my old self again as I stepped into my roles of shrew, control addict, and alcoholic.

The spiral only accelerated. Our house of cards collapsed into oblivion.

I fell deeply into codependent behaviors, into profound darkness, and was drinking more than ever before. Every day, I told myself I wouldn't drink, or at least wouldn't drink as much, but it only got worse.

I kept a flask in my car, taking a shot before leaving work because my job, once my haven, had become completely toxic. By the time I got home, I would pour a huge glass of wine and walk the dog, and by bedtime, I had consumed two bottles or more. That became my norm, the way I coped with a life I didn't like and certainly never, ever dreamed of.

My drinking was drowning out my Higher Self, and part of me had already given up hope. Hope for my son. Hope for my marriage. Hope for me.

When Alex turned 18, I had to find a way to get him out of the house. It had become too uncomfortable and toxic for everyone. By then, Bodhi had started using pot regularly. He looked better from the outside, but inside he was carrying the weight of our family's heaviness in his own ways.

Rich and I bickered constantly, yet we had no real connection. He buried himself in work and sports. I just checked out.

I had already left once and didn't think I could leave again. Even though my life felt like it was falling apart and my marriage wasn't what I had hoped for, it didn't seem to make sense to do anything different. When I came back, I had told myself that if it collapsed, I could walk away without guilt. But now I didn't even have the strength to walk away.

So I drank more and more until I was regularly blacking out, unable to remember conversations. At friends' dinner parties, I would repeat stories I had already told earlier in the evening, not realizing it. The boys would remind me of things I had said or tell me things I couldn't recall because I had blacked out.

Blood work from my doctor triggered an emergency room visit. I sat there and listened as Rich told the ER doctor I was an alcoholic. My alcoholic husband was the one expressing concern about my drinking. The tables had turned. By then, he had actually started drinking less, pouring himself into a new obsession with paddleboarding.

Meanwhile, my work environment was horrendous, and I lived in fear for Alex. He was out on his own, using massive amounts of drugs and drinking heavily. I had thought he would do better once he was out of our home, but instead, he was sinking deeper into his own addiction and the impossible complexity of trying to find your way as a grownup.

I had failed. I had failed my family, and I had failed myself. I journaled repeatedly about regret, remorse, and wanting to redo things. I did not understand the weight of my suffering and how to let go of control. **I did not understand that we, as a family, were all on our own journeys. I didn't realize that I would need to turn my attention inward and find a new way to see the world and people around me in order to begin healing from what felt like a painful and difficult life.**

My journal entry for October 3, 2014:

I want a do-over sometimes. I don't know how I am here today. What is my purpose here on the planet? What is the point? What are we doing here? Sometimes I think I could end my life today and be grateful for the release of pain.

I'm not sure exactly where I would make the changes, but I can't help feeling like I want a chance to do it differently. If this is my destiny, why have I gotten this one? Why has my life gotten so small? Where did my endless creative spirit go? Where did my hope and belief and humanity go? How do I make peace with this, that this is my life?

How can I get through this without losing complete hope? How do I find my way? How can I remember or discover who I am? Who have I become? Who am I, and how have I become so lost? How can I be the best person I can be in this lifetime? And how do I find myself again?

Do I deserve to actually want to live this life I am in? I can't help feeling like I failed all of this. I can't help but feel forgotten and that I've lost my way.

This was my ordinary world and my life before recovering my soul. This was the darkness I had to walk through before I could find my way back to the light, before I could remember who I truly was beneath all the pain, control, and addiction. Before I could begin the real journey of recovering my soul.

But here's what I know now that I didn't know then: Every moment of that pain was preparing me for awakening. Every broken dream, every failed attempt to control my family, every night I drank myself into oblivion, it was all leading me to the moment when the pain of staying the same would finally become greater than my fear of change.

That moment was coming. And when it did, it would change everything.

Conclusion

This chapter has been the world I lived in before my healing and awakening and the years of darkness before I could even imagine having light in my life. My life was shaped by control, addiction, and the constant ache of not-enoughness.

Every broken dream, every desperate attempt to fix or manage the people I loved, and every night I drank myself numb was preparing me for a turning point I could not yet see: **The moment when the pain of staying the same became greater than my fear of change.**

That moment did come. And when it did, everything shifted. It was the beginning of my transformation and the real work of recovering my soul. A central piece of that awakening was Al-Anon detachment: learning that my sanity, my serenity, could not come from controlling anyone else. My healing had to begin inside of me.

I didn't know it then, but that practice of letting go, of releasing control with compassion, would become one of the strongest foundations for everything that followed.

If you've ever felt trapped in someone else's chaos, if you've ever used a drink, a behavior, or control itself just to survive the day, you are not alone. I've lived it. And I share more of that story, along with the tools that helped me let go and begin to heal, on the *Recover Your Soul* podcast. These episodes are companions on the path home and reminders that you are not broken and that your soul remembers the way.

https://recoveryoursoulbook.com/

C H A P T E R   2 :

Recognize Suffering

Sometimes our deepest pain is the doorway to our greatest awakening. - RH

Sometimes it takes an emergency room visit to wake us up. Sitting in that thin gown, I felt vulnerable and exposed. In that raw moment, reality shook me awake and I could no longer pretend I was OK.

Those are the moments that can stop you in your tracks, when you finally give yourself the grace to pause and ask, "Who is this? Is this really who I am? Is this who I want to be?"

I am grateful that in one of those moments, a measure of grace broke through the noise and allowed my Higher Self to whisper that there was another way.

At the same time, Rich was finding his own path back to himself. A lifelong surfer, he had rediscovered his love for the sport after a trip to Hawaii. Back in Colorado, he had found stand-up paddleboarding on the whitewater rivers, and it filled a void he had been missing. He threw himself into it, competing, traveling with Bodhi, joining whatever events he could. He loved the community. He loved the challenge. He loved the way it felt to do well.

But he also knew the toll alcohol was taking. The physical effects slowed him down. He wasn't at his best, and his sleep was poor and fragmented. One day he came to me and said, "I think we should quit drinking again."

This was a moment when our deepest pain could become the doorway to our greatest awakening.

For us, it was a wake-up call. This was the man I had wanted so desperately to be sober for so long, the man I had finally given up on, convinced he would never change. And then, when he finally wanted sobriety, I was the one who was afraid.

I was afraid to quit drinking because I was afraid of what that would mean for my life. I was afraid that if I actually healed, if I allowed myself to blossom, it might cost me everything I knew. It might mean giving up this marriage. It might mean truly detaching from the pain of what was happening with my son and learning to let him go. And if I did that, I didn't know who I would be or what I would do in the world.

I was stuck in the cycle of discontent and suffering. I didn't know what to do next, or who I would be if I chose a different way to experience my life, without numbing, without hiding. I was consumed with fear and doubt, caught in the grip of my small self.

The Voice of Something Greater

But there is this moment that happens, a moment of grace, when, regardless of whether you are caught up in addiction or simply a painful season of life, the Spirit reaches in and whispers:

"You are worth it. Your life is worth it. You are here to be the full expression of your soul self. You are not here to be small. You are not here to drown. You are here to thrive and to grow. Are you going to choose to wake up? Are you going to choose to live?"

Today, as a metaphysical minister, I believe we are given free will and the freedom to choose our lives and the paths we walk. The path will give us what we need to learn. It can be and likely will be difficult, but if we are willing, we can begin to see it as our unique challenge, a way through to our wholeness.

When we are ready to step fully into wholeness, into faith, and into a connection with something Greater Still, the way is there, waiting. It is always there, waiting, whether we realize it or not.

This is the moment we stand at a crossroads. One path leads back into familiarity and what we already know of the patterns, pain, and smallness we've exemplified for so long. The other path is unknown and uncertain and certainly more challenging, but it holds the possibility of freedom and growth.

The one thing we must all do is make a choice, and even not choosing is still a choice.

For me, the path came through my husband, the very man I had complained about for so long, the one whose addiction I had resented. He was the one pointing to that path. And though I resisted, I knew this was the change I had been afraid to hope for. It was my moment of grace.

My Higher Self reminded me that my life is worth living. Even if it meant walking away from everything I knew, I was strong enough, worthy enough, and valuable enough to make that decision. And in that quiet moment, my Higher Self spoke clearly: "Don't be afraid to burn it all down and rise from the ashes."

The Song That Spoke My Truth

One of the bright spots in my life was the band Rich and I played in for about eight years. We often performed at our spiritual center and at small concerts. My dad had been a musician when I was growing up, and he always made sure I had a guitar. But I never really learned to play until I was about 30, when I finally took a lesson from someone at my church and learned the first five basic chords.

I began writing simple songs, and the amazing musicians in our band transformed them into something more complex and special. I sang, Rich played drums, and those were some of our happiest times together. The band was called Spirit Rising, and creating music with the people who joined and left that group over the years represented some of my most cherished memories.

When Rich came to me with this idea of sobriety, a chorus immediately came into my mind: "I know you're calling for me, why am I so afraid?" I could feel that Spirit was calling for me, and I was indeed afraid. Writing songs had been a way for me to process my feelings and share my heart. As the chorus and verses formed in my mind as I contemplated sobriety, it was as if my Higher Self were reminding me to listen to the calling.

I eventually recorded the song, published it on all the music streaming platforms, and even created a music video. "Calling for Me" by Rachel Harrison, on YouTube. You can find it here:

https://www.recoveryoursoul.net/music
"Calling for Me" By Rachel Harrison

I believe this is the whisper of our Higher Self, the voice of the soul, and the breath of Spirit: I know you are calling for me. Source, Spirit, God, or whatever name you give it, it is always calling for us. Calling us to be well, to be whole, to live as the full expression of who we truly are. Yet I was afraid to leave what I knew, even when what I knew was pain.

Psychology tells us that the primitive brain will cling to the familiar hurt rather than risk the unknown. But as souls, we came here for more than survival. **We came for the fullness of experience and for the chance to hear and answer the call of our soul.**

The Frog in Boiling Water

My journal entry for April 22, 2013:

> *The frog in the boiling water. We sit as it gets hotter and hotter, boiling only to kill us as we get used to it. I am the frog.*

*I feel completely lost. I feel almost numb when I think about
what's happening with our family.*

This journal entry is about the story of how frogs will allow themselves
to be boiled to death. The water heats so gradually that they don't realize it's killing them. I think when we begin to look at psychology and
spirituality, we can see the same truth in ourselves.

As human beings, we are conditioned to stay safe, to stay small, and
to endure difficulty. But in reality, that endurance can become the slow
boil that destroys us.

As spiritual beings, we are called to so much more. There is always
more available to us than we often see or understand. It is always there,
waiting but we must ask to receive it. Awakening often comes when
we hit the wall, when we find ourselves in a place so dark and painful
that it feels unbearable. Yet that very moment is also a message: We
are ready. Ready to do whatever it takes, ready to leap from the boiling
water, ready to heal.

In addiction, this is the turning point. Lasting change requires that
readiness. It demands the willingness to change and the courage to do
whatever it takes, including climbing out of the boiling water.

The Gift of Thailand

For Rich's 50th birthday in 2016, he went to Fiji for a month on his own
to meet up with some surfer friends. It was his dream trip, something
that had been on his bucket list for years. I was excited for him to go on
a couple of different levels.

First, of course, I wanted him to have the experience, a month
where he could fully connect with the ocean and be a surfer without
the responsibilities of family. But on a more selfish level, I also wanted
him to go because it gave me permission to want something similar for
myself someday.

So when my mom invited me to join her on a trip to Thailand, I felt
I could finally say yes to a trip that didn't include Rich or the boys. My
mom had always been a world traveler, taking big trips every few years.

That started when I was 8 years old, when she went to India for three months, leaving me with my grandmother.

That trip turned out to be wonderful for her, but it was a core trauma for me, something I will talk about later. Since that first trip in 1978, she has enjoyed traveling the world.

So in January of 2018, my mom, Lynda, and I set off for three weeks in Thailand and Myanmar. I knew this was going to be a life-changing trip. I decided I would use this time to detox, and that when I returned, I would commit to AA and sobriety.

I don't think my mom had any idea of the depth of my addiction, since I had kept it so well hidden. She had been worried about me for a long time, but she has always been naturally detached. Throughout my life, she let me have my own experiences with minimal control, which is fascinating given that I became such a control addict myself. That was never how she interacted with me.

As I prepared for the trip, I packed two one-gallon Ziploc baggies filled with mini bottles of vodka. Although I had three weeks to slowly taper off, I didn't want to be without alcohol: the true sign of an addict.

We set off on our trip. I weighed the heaviest I ever had in my life. I look back at pictures, and I'm bloated from alcohol. My face was round, and my system was not healthy, as the blood work from my most recent hospital visit had clearly indicated.

Again, a moment of grace, that whisper from my Higher Self that said, "It's time for something else, Rachel." And regardless of what happens on the other side, this was about being ready to choose myself and saving my own life.

Stepping Away from the Chaos

The trip was amazing. It gave me space to step away from a life that had grown complicated and painful. Before I left, Rich and I made an agreement that there would be minimal contact. I so desperately needed to get away. I needed a complete break.

And so I allowed myself to be guided. I stepped fully into my mom's world. As a Buddhist, she wanted to explore spiritual sites, temples, and museums. This was what she did on her trips. As a historian, spiritual practitioner, and artist, she immersed herself in the culture and the people. Aside from the time we lived in Europe when I was a senior in high school, I had never really traveled with her.

We flew into Bangkok and were immediately immersed in the city's vibrant atmosphere. What she didn't know was that tucked in my bag was enough alcohol to slowly detox, just enough each day to keep me from going into withdrawal. Thankfully, I didn't experience DTs, but I knew how dangerous it could be to quit suddenly.

But I wasn't only withdrawing from alcohol. I was withdrawing from the chaos and pain of my family. I was withdrawing from the daily intensity of a job that had become unhealthy and toxic. I was detoxing from the obsession with making sure everybody was OK, carrying the belief that it was somehow my responsibility.

I was detoxing from the patterns that kept me constantly on high alert and in fear. I was detoxing from my fear for Alex, from what was happening in his life, and from his addiction. I was detoxing from the life I had helped create and could no longer bear.

The First Glimpse of Freedom

What struck me almost immediately, not long after I arrived, was a sudden and startling awareness: My family could live without me. They would be OK without me. They weren't going to die or starve without me hovering, making sure every need was met. They were going to be all right.

That realization was its own moment of clarity, its own awakening. It was inspiration enough to show me that I could step away and let them handle things. Whatever happened, it belonged to them.

This was the beginning of letting go of control. The beginning of seeing that I was powerless over everything outside of myself. And it was also the first time I honestly admitted I was powerless over alcohol. I now had to admit that what I had accused Rich for so many years was true about myself. The trip gave me space to detox, but, at the same time, the obsession with drinking was still evident, still frightening.

I was powerless over alcohol, and I was powerless over my family, powerless over what they were doing at home, how they felt, and what was happening with them. And yet in that powerlessness came an enormous sense of freedom, the first real freedom I had felt in years. I didn't have to worry about them every moment. I could finally let them go.

Finding Myself in Sacred Places

My mom and I wandered the streets of Bangkok and Chiang Mai, visiting temples, museums, and shops. Then we flew to Myanmar to visit the Shwedagon Pagoda, a magnificent Buddhist temple. The grounds shimmered with golden towers encircling a vast golden dome, hundreds of Buddhas watching over the people as they chanted and prayed. And there, in that place, I found myself.

It was as if, in a flash, I remembered who I was. I remembered the parts of myself I had long locked away while trying to fix everybody else. My Higher Self opened. Time seemed to stand still as I circumambulated the temple, moving in step with the others. In that moment, there was no small self. I began to glimpse my true Self, the soul of me that was not the wife, mother, caretaker, or peacemaker. Just the essence of my wholeness.

I felt a sense of completeness that I had forgotten in the chaos of the last few years. For a brief moment, everything fell away, and I could see clearly.

I understood then that I needed to change my life. I was ready to awaken. I was ready to get sober for me, to save my life. I saw how much of my dissatisfaction and suffering had stemmed from the beliefs and stories I had chosen to live by and the way I was perceiving my life and everything in it.

On this trip, I experienced something new: I was able to relax, have fun, and be easygoing. I was able to be an enjoyable travel partner and to let go of control. My mom had planned our trip, and I could just let things be as they were. I realized how much I had been doing, how much I had been trying to control, and how the anxiety and fear had led me off course.

I had lost my way.

I could see my unhealthy marriage, and for the first time in a long time, I could clearly see my part in it. I could feel how the woman on this trip, lighthearted, happy, and easy, was not the woman who lived in my home. I saw all the complex layers of personalities and the battlefield we had been fighting on together. But more than anything, I saw my part.

I felt compassion for myself and for my family. I was ready for change. I was willing to do whatever it took to find a new way. That was the beginning of my awakening, the beginning of my transformation.

Slowly, over those three weeks, I let go of the part of me that was afraid. I opened to the whisper: "I know you're calling for me. I know you're calling for me, Spirit. I know you're calling for me, Life. I know you're calling for me, Higher Self. And I am ready. I want so desperately to step into that place. I'm ready."

By the end of the trip, I was down to one or two big Thailand beers a day. The little vodka shooters I had brought were long gone. I felt relaxed. I felt at ease. I felt free. And I was finally ready to let go of the demon of alcohol that had consumed me for so long.

I had just turned 48 years old. I had once promised myself that I would have my life together by the time I was 40, but that promise had slipped away. Now, for the first time, I felt hope. I trusted that something was calling for me. I believed in it. I felt a faith deeper than I had ever known before.

I was grateful for the gift this trip had given me, half a world away from my family. I had to choose myself. I had to save myself.

The Last Dance with My Old Friend

As I stepped onto the airplane, ready to return to the chaos, back into what felt like the lion's den, I had my last drinks. I was grateful that international flights offered free wine and beer. I wasn't out of control, but I kept calling the flight attendants back to my seat again and again for another glass of white wine until they finally stopped serving me.

Then I sent my mom to the galley to bring me the last few glasses.

At one point, when a flight attendant passed by and I asked for another glass of wine, she said, "I have never served so much alcohol as I have on this flight." Whether she meant it for me or in general, I felt the truth of it deep inside.

I knew this was the end. These were the last moments I would share with what had once felt like an old friend, a friend that had turned on me, that was no longer a solution but a poison harming me in every way. I was ready to let it go.

The Moment of Truth

When we landed in Denver, Rich picked us both up at the airport. After 30 hours of international travel, with a layover in Tokyo, I was haggard and hazy from all the wine and the time zone changes. I wanted to be excited to see him, to share the glow of my trip and the new awareness I carried of my readiness to be sober.

It was the very thing he had been asking for. But the old patterns were there waiting. I felt Rich's tension the moment he pulled up to the curb. It was that familiar and uncomfortable tension I had walked on eggshells around for more than 20 years.

Ten minutes into the drive, Rich launched into how upset he was with Alex, detailing everything our son had done wrong over the last three weeks. And in that instant, everything came flooding back. The pain and suffering. The years of difficult memories. The reality of our family's dysfunction. The complexity and the discontent of a father with his son.

But I had made a decision. February 10, 2018, would be my sober day. **I had decided I was willing to do whatever it took to save my life.**

Then something powerful happened. As I sat there listening to Rich rant, weighed down by his dissatisfaction with Alex, I quietly said the Serenity Prayer. But this time I felt it in a way I never had before.

***

God, grant me the serenity to accept the things I cannot change....

(I felt those words in my heart. I understood them.)

The courage to change the things I can....

(That was me. To change me. and whether I stayed an addict.)

And the wisdom to know the difference.

(I could see it so clearly: The only person I could change was me.)

***

In my travel-worn delirium, a moment of grace opened. I realized I had to be willing to walk away from everything if that's what it took to save myself. I had to be willing to do whatever it took to be happy. For three weeks, I had tasted freedom and happiness. I had felt it in my heart, in my body, in my soul, and I wanted that to be my life.

I could no longer tolerate the dysfunction. I had to look at myself with honesty and courage and change the only thing I could: me.

Choosing Myself for the First Time

And so I walked back into the rooms of AA. Not for Rich this time, but for me. Not with the hope of making my husband stop drinking, but with a deep knowing that this was about my recovery, my addiction, and my life. This was the first step in reclaiming my life and becoming my awakened self.

And it was different this time. I sat down in the chair, ready to save myself.

Then I spoke the words I had resisted for so long:

"My name is Rachel, and I am an alcoholic."

For the first time, with clarity and honesty, I could see that I was powerless over alcohol and that it had dominated and destroyed my life for more than 20 years. Not just Rich's drinking, but my drinking. I was ready, at last, to truly take the first step and admit that I was powerless.

They say in the 12-Step principles of AA that this is the only step you have to take with every ounce of your being. All the others are suggestions, a path to healing. But the first step brings freedom. It breaks the false belief that you can manage it and opens up the willingness to do whatever it takes to get well.

In that meeting, with profound grace, the obsession was lifted. I was ready for change. I was ready to wake up. I was ready to heal, ready to live, ready to open to my Higher Self and remember my wholeness.

Working the Steps in Your Own Life

Recover Your Soul - STEP 1

1. Ready for Awakening
Recognize Suffering: **Become aware that your dissatisfaction and suffering are rooted in your current perceptions, beliefs, patterns, and stories.** *Acknowledge the Need for Change:* **Understand that this awareness is the first step toward awakening and transformation.**

***

This chapter has been about awakening and about the moment when I could no longer deny the truth of my life and had to face myself honestly. In the quiet clarity that came after so much chaos, I saw that change had to begin with me. Not with Rich, not with my sons, not with my family, but with me.

Step 1 of the Recover Your Soul Process is where denial ends and surrender begins. It's where we stop pointing outward and begin to look inward, where we release the false belief that we can control anyone else and finally take responsibility for our own healing. We recognize that our dissatisfaction and suffering are rooted in our current perceptions, beliefs, patterns, and stories, and we acknowledge that this awareness is the first step toward transformation.

It is no exaggeration to say that the decision to heal, which came from this step, saved my life.

Awakening is not a one-time event. It's a practice, a journey of learning to see differently and to live differently. Each moment offers us the opportunity to choose awareness over denial, honesty over hiding, and courage over comfort.

If this part of my story has resonated with you, I invite you to listen to these Recover Your Soul podcast episodes that build on the themes from this chapter:

Podcasts About Ready for Awakening

https://recoveryoursoulbook.com/

CHAPTER 3

Letting Go

The most radical act of love I've ever practiced is letting go of trying to fix the people I love. - RH

Breaking the habit of being yourself is not an easy thing to do. Although I was deeply committed to both AA and Al-Anon and attending weekly meetings, working the steps with my sponsor, saying daily prayers, building new sober friendships, and finding success in releasing my alcohol addiction, I was also uncovering something deeper. I was beginning to see the habitual patterns, beliefs, and stories that had shaped the way I showed up in my life, and the pain that came with them.

In the 12 Steps, admitting you are powerless and that your life has become unmanageable is the foundation of recovery. My life had become unmanageable, and I was finally ready to admit I was powerless over alcohol.

That admission became a new freedom. I could feel the truth of it in my bones. For so long, I tried to outrun it and deny it, but finally surrendering allowed me to move through the other steps with greater honesty. It deepened my understanding of the 12 Steps as more than a program; they were, and are, a spiritual path to healing.

It was as if everything I had ever studied in Unity Church I attended everything I had absorbed as the daughter of a Buddhist, everything I had underlined and highlighted in the books I read and listened to, all of it began to come together. The pieces of the puzzle started to come together. I could see more deeply, hear from a new perspective, and understand more fully because I was willing to surrender.

To admit that I was powerless over alcohol was to release a burden I had carried for more than 20 years. It didn't mean I didn't miss it. I did. I missed the ritual, the habit. But my desire for happiness, for a new way of living, was stronger. I cared so deeply about this new experience of healing that I was willing to do whatever it took to save my life.

The Harder Truth: Powerlessness over Others

But when I walked into the rooms of Al-Anon, that same first step of admitting that I was powerless over someone else's addiction and unhealthy behaviors and admitting that my life had become unmanageable because of my attempts to control or change them was harder for me to accept at first than admitting I was an alcoholic.

I remember sitting in those rooms, hearing the words and stories of people sharing their experience, strength, and hope. I heard my own stories, complaints, and fears spilling out of my mouth, but I couldn't seem to detach or let go of the desire to fix what felt broken. What if I let my son die? What if his depression takes him? What if his addiction claims his life?

I carried such a heavy sense of responsibility for his well-being. I believed I had to find the solutions to make it different than it was. I was in so much pain over his addiction and mental health struggles, in so much pain over his sadness and turmoil. With so many difficult situations swirling around us, I wanted desperately to find a way to help him, to fix him, and to save him.

When Alex went into residential treatment at 16, I remember sitting in the waiting room during an early visit. I overheard the director say to someone else, "It's not if a child relapses, it's when." I was furious. Angry. Upset. Confused. I was paying for them to fix my son. I wanted this to be the thing that would change him, heal him, and save him.

If he could be healed, and fixed, then our family could be fixed. I had been holding on to this belief since he was in middle school. It seemed so simple, and I thought that this would be the answer to all of our dysfunction and the years of upset.

Yet sitting in the rooms of Al-Anon, the awareness became clear: I was powerless over someone else's addiction. Just as my own recovery required the recognition that I can never drink again and that I can never put a drop of alcohol to my lips because it will always take over, no matter how well I may seem. In that same light, I began to see the truths of Al-Anon for the first time. To recover from my codependency and people-pleasing, I would need to let go of my illusion of control. That was the only way to find recovery.

So slowly, one day at a time, I became open to the truth that I was powerless over everything outside of myself. I was so afraid of losing my son on so many different levels, but I was beginning to understand: I was powerless over his addiction, his choices, his happiness, and his life.

The Beginning of Release

Something began to change. My heart began to loosen. I started to truly hear the words being spoken in those rooms. I could read the Al-Anon literature with new eyes, from a perspective that helped me understand my suffering. I realized how tightly I was clinging and attached to his journey, his pain, and his experience, almost as if it were my own.

It would be a long time before I fully understood the layers of healing ahead of me, but this was the beginning. Just one tiny shift, one fraction of a step, and my grip of fear began to loosen. I started to see that my need to be on top of everything wasn't only about my sons or my husband.

I was trying to change and fix everything around me. And if I was honest, I believed that was my job. I was exhausted. My life had become unmanageable.

Control at Work

In 2010, when I turned 40, I began working as the office manager of a home care agency. It was during my first sobriety. It was a job where I felt truly loved, seen, and recognized for the wide range of skills I had gathered over the years. It felt good to be in a place that was of service in so many ways.

We were helping clients live their final years with dignity and love. We were giving caregivers steady work and the chance to share their gifts of service and compassion. We nicknamed ourselves the Love Boat, and that's exactly how it felt. Healthy. Happy. A place of peace when everything at home felt so out of control. Work gave me a sense of security, safety, and purpose.

Many times, when my family was unraveling, going into that office was the only place where I felt safe, where I could breathe, and where I could simply be myself. It was a reprieve from the chaos and pain of my home life.

But looking back, I can see that from the very beginning I carried with me the impulse to "improve" things and to take charge, to make it better. I also longed to be noticed, to be acknowledged for my efforts, so I could feel valuable and worthy.

What I didn't see then was the unconscious belief driving me: that it was my job to improve, fix, and find solutions... control. Yes, I had important skills and a kindness of heart that benefited the company, but beneath it was a blind spot: an unhealthy need to fix and save, born from my addiction to control itself.

When Rich and I separated and I started drinking again, things began to slip. I wasn't living the recovery work that had once given me peace during my three years of sobriety. I was caught in the fog and distorted vision that come with addiction, falling back into the small, fearful ego self of being reactive, defensive, consumed with hurt and the desire to find an answer to fix that pain.

And although there were still moments when my Higher Self showed up, more and more often, my unhealthy, unhappy self took charge.

I grew increasingly controlling of everything outside of me, although I didn't recognize it as control. I thought I was helping. I thought I was making things better. I thought I knew the better way. A friend of mine used to tease me about always having the "right way" and being bossy, but I didn't hear her honesty. I dismissed it, clinging to the belief that I had the correct solutions and that I was helping people.

I believed I had so much to offer, so much to give from my big heart that only wanted everyone to be happy and not have to go through hardship. I thought my ideas were good solutions, that I could fix things. What I couldn't see was that this, too, was control. I didn't see that in my efforts to fix and save, I wasn't allowing others to be on their own journey, to have their own experiences, and that included their own pain, challenge, and suffering.

The Family Battlefield

It felt like it was my job to take care of everyone, to head off any upsets, to keep the peace, and to find the solutions. All of the difficulties that we were having in our home could disappear if I could just sprinkle some sort of stardust over it, some sort of well-being magic, some sort of amount of love and healing. If we could just stop hurting each other, then everything would be OK.... I could be OK.

I wanted to do everything I could to make that happen, so I inserted myself in every conversation. I triangulated and played the role of referee and peacekeeper. I tried to create an environment that kept everybody from being upset. I tried to stay ahead of it all and make sure that I was heading off any difficulties or painful situations. I was on high alert at all times, attending to everyone and everything.

As I worked with Step One in Al-Anon and saw my real issue of codependency, people-pleasing, and the level of my control addiction, there was a shift and an awareness and a willingness to make a new choice.

I began to slowly realize that everything I had learned in my spiritual studies and everything I had been absorbing at my Unity Church for so long had been offering the truth all along. But I hadn't heard it with my heart, only my head. I was too consumed with trying to be a good person and taking on the roles of helper, fixer, and peacemaker. I would eventually see that I was actually in the throes of my deeper addiction and control issues. Even my drinking was an attempt to control my own pain.

Addiction means a compulsive behavior or the compulsive and consuming thoughts we can't stop. The worry that was in my mind, spinning constantly around everything and everyone. I so wanted it to be different. I was suffering from wanting it to be something other than what it was, and I was in pain.

I hadn't been in a place where I thought I could get help or even ask for it. I thought I was alone in this. I was taking on the responsibility for everything and everyone. I felt the weight of the world on my shoulders. I felt the weight of my family, especially my children, on my shoulders and in my heart.

The relationship between Rich and Alex had only grown more complicated and difficult as the years passed. When I had left Rich and moved out of the house with Alex, there was so much pain and conflict. I believed I was saving us from the turmoil and dysfunction that had taken over our home.

Rich often reflected that because I was raised by a single Buddhist mother in a household without conflict, a blessing in so many ways, but maybe a curse in others, I had never learned how to navigate conflict. I didn't understand what it meant to fight and then move on. I wanted peace and ease all the time.

I didn't understand that conflict and upset were part of normal life. My tolerance for it was so low that anything beyond calm felt intolerable.

Rich, on the other hand, had grown up surrounded by conflict and intensity. He was reacting from his own learned roles and defenses, and the two of us simply couldn't relate to each other's baselines and argued over who was "right."

The relationship he had with Alex was equally painful. It was hard on both of them, but at the time I couldn't see Rich's pain. I could only see my son's pain, and I believed it was my job to protect him from who I thought was the aggressor. There were many times when Rich said to me, "If it came down to choosing between me and Alex, you'd choose Alex." And every time, I answered, "I absolutely would. I will always choose my son." That was the battlefield that had been created between us.

We were no longer on the same team. We were on opposing sides, locked in a constant fight for control, fighting for who was right and without any awareness that we could both hold our own truths and that neither of us had to be right or wrong. We didn't have that language yet. We didn't have that understanding yet. More importantly, I didn't have that understanding yet and was digging into the battle and making Rich the enemy, believing I was protecting my children.

It was a constant struggle, and that struggle only made the relationship with Rich and Alex more complicated and painful for everyone.

Learning to Listen

Our communication had been what drove us to marriage counseling in our very first years together, and it was still one of the most painful and difficult parts of our relationship. It was the battlefield where all our unhealed wounds met.

Years earlier, during our first sobriety, we had read The Four Agreements by Don Miguel Ruiz together. The teachings of

- Be impeccable with your word
- Don't take things personally
- Don't make assumptions
- Always do your best

had been a glimmer of awareness at the time. We could see the wisdom in them, but we weren't ready to understand what was underneath our defensiveness. In our woundedness, these beautiful values seemed too far off to actually live from.

The truth was, there had been a slow erosion of trust between us that had created a profound lack of safety in our marriage. We each felt like we couldn't be open with our hearts. We were always on the defense, always braced for the next hurt. Neither of us felt heard or understood. We had both contributed to this erosion over the years, each responding to our own pain with the only defensive patterns we knew.

A friend of ours who had been walking the recovery path for many years could see how much we were struggling. She was kind, grounded, and deeply committed to the principles of the program. She offered to meet with both of us to work on our communication using the structure and rules of a 12-step meeting. We said yes immediately.

She would meet with us in our living room, notebook and timer in hand. The rules were simple: Keep the focus on yourself. No interrupting. No cross-talk. Five minutes each to share while she gently redirected us away from blame and back to ourselves.

In our very first meeting, she made a statement that struck me deeply, though I couldn't fully absorb it at the time through my own suffering. She said, simply and truthfully, "You don't have a safe marriage."

She was right. With her there as moderator, I could see our pattern clearly: constant attack and defense. The emotional battlefield was laid bare.

I was always waiting to point out what Rich was doing wrong, convinced my guidance came from love and a desire for things to be better. But as I would share what I thought he needed to change, Rich would hear it as an attack. He would become defensive, talking over me, explaining until I felt guilty for my own feelings, completely unheard and misunderstood. If I didn't shut down completely, I would go on the attack, full of blame and anger from a place that felt out of control.

When we drank, these fights were devastating, ending in days of silent treatment, never resolved. Just slowly let go over time, the hurt still sitting there between us.

This wasn't about one of us being "bad." We were each using the only defensive patterns we had learned over our lives. We each felt unheard and misunderstood, over and over again. Both of us were trapped in our own forms of control, desperately trying to be seen, to be understood, and to feel safe.

Working with our friend gave us both a chance to share our full thoughts and begin to create safety in our communication. Safety didn't mean the other had to agree with us, but that there was space to share our hearts without interruption or defense.

As I learned to listen, really listen, for just five minutes, I heard something I hadn't allowed myself to hear before. Rich would share with profound awareness of his own feelings and behaviors. He could see openings, places where he was beginning to shift, and new ways of understanding situations, including his relationship with Alex. When I wasn't interrupting with my solutions, I could hear him processing his own pain, his own fears, and his genuine desire to do better.

And in the space I had to talk, when Rich was required to sit quietly and just listen, I began to share my own deeper feelings. Not my criticisms of him, but the truth beneath them: my sense of responsibility for everything, the emptiness in my soul that was driving my behaviors, and the fear that kept my heart closed.

Because we had separated before, Rich didn't want that to happen again. I, too, was motivated to create safety in our relationship and get off the emotional battlefield. I wanted to learn to be a better listener and to actually share myself when he was ready to listen.

It only took a few of those meetings to see our unhealthy pattern clearly and to make a decision together to try to do better as a commitment to a healthier relationship.

I would love to report that our communication issues were resolved easily from these awarenesses. They were not. Old patterns don't disappear overnight, and the intensity of what we were facing as a family didn't magically dissolve. Our communication began to improve, slowly and imperfectly. It remains a continued work in progress.

But it was a turning point. A shift from unconsciously hurting each other to consciously trying to be kind, compassionate, and curious.

What I learned in those sessions was something that would become foundational to my healing: the most powerful thing I could do was get out of the way and let go of control. Stop trying to fix, manage, or correct. Just listen. Just witness. Just allow it, not just for him, but for myself too. **This was not about blame or judgment. It was about being willing to see the situation as it was and give each person a chance to learn and grow while letting go of control and desired outcomes as the focus of the healing.**

I was beginning to understand that in theory. Living it would be my continued journey to recover my soul.

The Revelation

As I sat in the rooms of Al-Anon, in that safe recovery space, I listened to a new kind of language: words and stories that carried power, honesty, and transformation. I heard people talk about detaching, about letting go, about finding peace in places I had only known struggle, conflict, and pain.

And slowly, I began to see my part. I wasn't just a bystander. I had been a player in this painful drama, trying to control, fix, and manage what was never mine to hold. By triangulating and interfering, I had made already-complicated relationships even more entangled.

This wasn't the fault of one of us; it was the responsibility of all four of us.

I began to admit:

I was powerless over my family's addiction.

I was powerless over their relationships with each other.

I was powerless over how they spoke to each other.

I was powerless over the kind of father Rich chose to be to his sons.

I was powerless over how my sons responded to their father.

I was powerless over my children's choices and the way they showed up in their own lives.

I was powerless over my husband's anger and expectations.

I was powerless over Alex's and Bodhi's emotions and pain.

I was powerless over them, yet I was not powerless over me.

There was one therapy session we went to as a family during that time that has stayed with me. In that room, Bodhi spoke words I will never forget. He said his brother had always received all the attention and that I had been so focused on what was wrong with Alex that I had failed to see him and that he felt ignored. Left behind. And he was right.

So much of our family energy was spent circling the fire, staring at what wasn't working, that we sometimes forgot to see the whole room. We forgot to listen to each person's story. We forgot to ask what each heart needed. Instead, we zeroed in on the most obvious "problem" and placed it all on Alex, as if he alone carried the weight of our brokenness. But the truth was more complicated: we were a system.

We were a dysfunctional, alcoholic, codependent system. A family that loved each other fiercely and still caused each other immense pain. And that paradox has always struck me about how people can love so much and still wound each other so deeply. Every time I thought I was saving us, I was only adding to the wound.

I remember leaving Rich, convinced I was saving Alex. Later, I found a journal entry where Alex yelled at me that it was all my fault. How could I break up our family? How could I leave Dad? Why couldn't I make it better? His words sliced through me, because I had believed with my whole heart that I was doing the right thing.

Looking back now, I see how much control I was grasping for in every corner of our lives. I told myself it was because I wanted them to be happy. And yes, I wanted that desperately. But beneath it, the truth was sharper: I needed them to be OK so that I could be OK. My attempts to "save them" were, in reality, attempts to save myself from the unbearable discomfort of our life as it was. A friend had said to me, "You are only as happy as your least happy child." And that had become a badge of purpose for me. Because I had a child who was not happy, I believed for me to be happy, I had to find a way to fix this and make him happy... so I could at last be happy.

I couldn't see then what is so clear to me now. I only had my old and limited resources and tools for this very complex situation that was indeed painful and hard for everyone. All I had was myself, showing up with the only version of "best" I knew how to give. I can also see now that I was giving all my power away by needing and wanting everything outside of me to be OK so that I could be OK and I did not understand that I never had and never could have control of anything outside of myself. That freedom would come not from holding on tighter, but from learning to let go.

The Moment of Surrender

As Alex grew older, the dynamic between him and his father only grew more complicated. He had a voice now, and he used it as a weapon to hurt and fight back, oftentimes with force. There were fights, slammed doors, harsh words, and yelling flung back and forth. Emotional injuries on all sides. It was incredibly painful and sometimes frightening. It was exhausting. And it wounded my soul.

By then, Rich had begun employing Alex in a desperate attempt to take care of him, keeping him tethered at least by the security of a job. It was his way of trying to hold on to control and help a son who he saw going off the rails.

I remember one Al-Anon meeting in particular on a day when Alex and Rich had exploded at each other. The fighting, screaming, and repeated unhealthy patterns left me totally undone. My stomach was knotted, my heart heavy, and my head was just pounding. I sat there with the weight of it all pressing down on me, drowning in anxiety, swallowed by the thought that maybe there was no hope for our family.

But I didn't drink. I didn't numb. Instead, I chose my sobriety. I chose to stay awake, knowing it would be hard, my Higher Self reminding me it would be worth it. I chose to reach for the new tools I was learning: get to a 12-Step meeting, open a book, pray, and ask Spirit for help. So I went. I walked into an Al-Anon room because, at that moment, it was the only lifeline I had.

Something profound happened that day. It was a quiet turning point, a soft step forward. I walked in, found my chair, and just listened, simply there to witness others' stories. I didn't listen to fix, not to measure myself against anyone else, but in that circle, in that stillness, I forgot about my own family for a moment. I wasn't carrying Rich and Alex on my shoulders. It was just me.

And as I listened, my stomach unclenched. The throbbing in my head eased, and a calmness settled over me. In the presence of Al-Anon wisdom, I felt something shift: a release. I could admit it at last. I was powerless over them. Powerless over their choices, their battles, their pain. And in saying it, in letting it be true, I could finally breathe.

And the Serenity Prayer rose up in me, the prayer I was learning to understand and use to release the tension in my body and heart:

***

God, grant me the serenity to accept the things I cannot change….

(Everything – them, their situation, their feelings. I cannot change any of that. None of us can force change anything outside of ourselves.)

The courage to change the things I can…

(My way of seeing, my ability to stay present in the discomfort, and the small, steady choices I can make to heal myself.)

And the wisdom to know the difference.

***

But sometimes that line feels blurred and fuzzy. It feels tangled and sticky, like love itself is a net you can't slip free from. In that meeting, I realized how fiercely I loved them all. My husband. My sons, Alex and Bodhi. And Bodhi, especially, caught in the middle, trying so hard to be the peacemaker, holding our fragile family together with hugs and smiles, the heavy weight of the role we had given him in our family

He wanted so badly to lighten the tension, to smooth over the sharp edges, to be the good boy who could turn the storm into sunshine. Even then, I can see now, he was already learning his own codependent patterns and the people-pleasing behaviors that would follow him into adulthood and fuel his own addictions. It was his way of trying to make it all OK.

When I stepped out of that meeting, I had surrendered. I had touched a moment of grace where I could finally say, "Whatever it is for them, it is for them. I cannot control them. I am not responsible for them."

And in that surrender, peace settled in my heart, a peace deeper than anything I had felt before, maybe ever.

I knew I could and likely would go back home and find chaos waiting. But what I found instead astonished me: they were OK. Alex and Rich had actually talked, not screamed. The house was calm. And in that moment, I saw something I had never considered before: if I removed myself from trying to manage it all, maybe there was a chance for something new to grow between them. A chance that their relationship could unfold in ways I never would have scripted, not as I would have written it, but real nonetheless.

Right there, I made a promise to myself to get out of their relationship. To let it be theirs to shape, choose, and live in. It might not look like what I wanted, but it could be what they created together. And to this day, to the best of my ability, I have kept that promise.

The Shrew Moment

That day, I recognized something I had been blind to: I was powerless over their relationship. And from there, it became a kind of mantra:

I am powerless over everything outside of myself.

Once I let that truth in, I began to see just how many places I had been slipping my fingers into everything, convinced that I knew best for everyone and every situation.

I was talking about this recently with a friend, laughing about how far I had come. She said, "Remember when you used to get so upset about how they did the filing at your office manager job?" And she was right. Back then, it consumed me. I actually lost sleep over how papers were filed. It sounds absurd now, but I would get furious because I thought I had a better system.

Maybe it was a better way. But at what cost? I became difficult to work with, sharp-edged, resentful, and rigid. I wrapped my need for control in the disguise of "helping." I was taking my responsibility as a manager too seriously, stepping in where I was not invited. But the truth was simpler and harsher: I was trying to save everyone else so I didn't have to face what needed saving in me.

Now I see that we are all on our own spiritual journeys. Each of us is walking through layers of experience far beyond what anyone else can see or understand. How could I possibly know what is best for another soul's path or the path of an organization?

I was only just beginning to open to that idea back then. I had heard the sayings over the years: We are spiritual beings having a human experience. We are spiritual beings in a human body. I believed it, but didn't really understand it. I had been raised Buddhist, and I believed in reincarnation. I had some sense of the essence of a soul, but I couldn't quite grasp the unlimited nature of the teachings. Still, I was getting curious and could feel that my Higher Self was leading the way.

The truth was, I was deeply attached to my human experience of life and relationships. I was attached to my thoughts, my way of thinking, and the belief that if I could just help enough, fix enough, save enough, and then I could feel safe and be happy. I believed that happiness came from it all being OK on the outside.

In the end, all that need to control was really about my own emotional, physical, and spiritual safety. I began to realize that the grip I had on everything, the need to manage the outcome, was making me sick. It was draining the life out of me. It was making me miserable. My life had become unmanageable.

In Al-Anon, I finally heard the words that named it: We are sick with our obsession over someone else's sickness. We make ourselves ill trying to cure what we cannot change. **I was powerless over the choices others made. Powerless over whether they would get well or not. And slowly I was beginning to deeply understand: I was not responsible for fixing everything or everyone.**

In the midst of all this, I was immersed in my AA work. I had a sponsor, and together we read the Big Book one section at a time. I was working the 12 Steps. I was showing up at meetings, surrendering, and doing everything my sponsor told me to do.

And I began to recognize something uncomfortable: as much as I wanted to manage and control everything, I didn't actually enjoy it. Being so tightly wound, trying to make everything run smoothly was exhausting. It left me in an emotional battlefield with everything and everyone. I didn't want to live in opposition anymore. I was beginning to believe there had to be a better way.

In those 12-Step rooms, and through the deepening spiritual teachings from my Unity church, something inside me began to shift again, and I began to awaken even more. Slowly, the jigsaw puzzle of my life was taking on a different shape, a new clarity.

I began to see that there was far more happening beneath the surface than I had ever realized. My subconscious was carrying beliefs, stories, and patterns that shaped how I showed up. This wasn't because I was bad or unkind or nitpicky; I wanted so much to be good. But I had been operating from a place that was closed off, rigid, and tightly wound.

In my journal entry on February 19, 1997, I wrote:

> *I will place my thick wall around my heart for them and not allow them in. The world is not safe, and how can it be? I cannot trust anyone.*

My perception wasn't healed yet. It wasn't open. And that, more than anything, was what needed to shift.

At our Unity Church, we had prayer chaplains. One Sunday, after a service, Rich and I sat down and asked for a prayer because we had been bickering that morning. I don't remember most of the words, but somewhere in that prayer, our prayer chaplain said the word "shrew."

It struck me and shined light on a shadow in my subconscious. I was in a new state of awareness, now truly willing to look at myself instead of everyone else. And I had to admit that the word fit. I had been acting in a shrew-like way. Not nearly as bad as in the past, but still argumentative, nagging, visibly annoyed, and using old defense mechanisms to deal with my hurt.

In that moment of grace, something opened in me, and I saw it clearly: It didn't matter what I said. I could nitpick all day long. I could pour out kindness all day long. I could choose all the right words, and it still would not change the situation for what it was. **The only real change had to come from within me. I needed to shift how I showed up. And just as importantly, I needed to allow others in my life to be who they were and to accept situations for what they were.**

Even if that meant my husband and son didn't get along. Even if it meant Rich was not the father I had envisioned he would be. What if I let him be the father he was? What if I let Alex be the son, the young man, he was becoming in his own right? I was beginning to find the answers.

The Decision to Change

Once I made the decision to change and to finally see how I had been trying to control so many things, in so many places, I began to hear affirmation everywhere. I heard it in the AA and Al-Anon literature I read each day. I found it in the spiritual books I had been collecting for years and was now reading voraciously. The message was the same: surrender, let go of control, and admit that you are powerless as a way to take back your power and find peace.

And now I could see what was being taught by so many. Letting go wasn't a weakness. It wasn't giving up. It was a strength. It was allowing. It was acceptance. It was a path to wholeness.

And acceptance doesn't mean you have to like it. **To accept simply means you stop fighting with what is, and in that release, the suffering ends and you step off the battlefield.**

That's when I began to understand the Third Noble Truth of Buddhism, and it says that there is a way out of suffering. Our suffering comes from the clinging, the desperate wanting, the demand that life be different from what it is. But there is a way to let go of that illusion of control. There is a way to release the suffering.

I realized I had been confusing feelings with suffering. Feelings are valid and important. They are meant to be felt, and they have a purpose.

But it's when we try to control them, to manage and manipulate them, to bend them to our will, that we suffer. The teaching that became alive in me was this: Feel the feelings fully, but let go of the need to control the outcome.

The Third Noble Truth, that there is a way out of suffering and that it is a spiritual path, suddenly became more than a teaching. It became a lifeline.

As I was walking the path of letting go of control, I wrote a song about loving the people in my life just as they are.

"Love Each Other" by Rachel Harrison
https://www.recoveryoursoul.net/music

The Job Collapse and Rebirth

By 2019, things at my job as an office manager had become incredibly complicated. When I first got sober, my sponsor had told me I couldn't leave that job for a year, which is a very traditional piece of recovery wisdom: Don't make any big moves in the first year. And although it had been a safe and even enjoyable place for me for many years, that had changed.

The environment grew painful and difficult, and I had to admit that part of it was my own control addiction. I had shown up in ways that contributed to the unhealthiness, pushing and forcing, trying to shape it into something I thought it should be.

At one point, I even thought I wanted to step into the director role when it opened up. But then everything blew up. It was one of those moments when you think, "This is what I want. I'll make it happen," and then the Universe steps in with a hard no. Everything collapsed on every level.

When I stepped back and let my Higher Self speak, the truth was, I didn't want to be there anymore, and they didn't want me there either. I had to leave, and I could see how tightly I had been holding on not just to controlling the environment, but to controlling my next step, controlling who I thought I was, and controlling how I was supposed to show up in the world. I was still chasing approval from the outside and was attached to the illusion that I had any power over any of it.

Everything in my life seemed to be shedding at once. Old patterns, old expectations, old ways of holding on. I was slowly and painfully learning to let people be where they were, to stop gripping so tightly, to let them live their own story, and to stop fixing and saving.

In the very same season, my job was unraveling, and with it came a flood of feelings I had buried for so long. Grief. Fear. Anger. And then, strangely, a kind of release. I stood in the middle of it all, uncertain, stripped down, with no clear sense of what I was supposed to do next, but I was beginning to understand that surrender was the path forward.

The moment I finally let go and decided I was ready to leave, I got a call from a headhunter offering me another job. It was one of those unmistakable moments of grace when you realize that if you let go of control and admit you're powerless and turn it over to something Greater, you will be held and cared for. You will be led to where you are meant to be.

I had never fully trusted that before. Even after years on a spiritual path, I carried the belief that I alone had to do everything, that I was responsible for holding up the entire weight of my life. I didn't believe that there was anyone there for me and that I had to do it all on my own.

And yet, within weeks of my nine-year job unraveling, the Universe lifted me up and out and placed me somewhere new, in a job that was, quite honestly, boring and safe. It was a temp position in the HR Department of a large corporation.

I sat at a desk in a windowless closet, doing data entry. And it turned out to be one of the greatest gifts I could have received at that time. I had come out of a complex, painful, exhausting environment and landed in a space that was simple, clear, and predictable. I knew exactly what was expected of me: when to show up, how long to stay, and what my role was. The work wasn't complicated, the people were kind, and best of all, they knew nothing of my life, my history, or the storm I had just walked through.

I had nothing to control here, and I felt relief. I felt freedom. I felt grace and gratitude. I was making less money, but it didn't matter because I knew this was right for me. Of course, the old urge to control still rose up with that familiar voice that wanted to step in and "improve" things. It had been my pattern for so long. But now, I simply noticed it and let it go.

I was grateful that in this new situation, I was not in charge, and it gave me space to explore my own inner landscape, the complex and difficult feelings I had pushed away for so many years. Instead of acting on the urge to be a leader and fixer, I just watched it pass through me.

I began to see that control was like a well-worn road in my mind, a neural pathway I had traveled so many times that it felt like the only way forward. The pavement was smooth from overuse, the signs all pointing in one direction: manage it, fix it, save them, control it. For years, I didn't even realize there were other paths available. **It never occurred to me that I could step off that familiar road and start carving a new trail.**

At first, the new way was rough and overgrown, like hacking through brush in a wilderness. It felt unnatural, even dangerous. But little by little, each time I chose surrender over control, a new trail appeared. Each time I released instead of gripped, it became easier to walk.

I was learning that I could hand it over to something Greater Still and was not alone in this. I was powerless over alcohol. I was powerless over my family's addictions. I was powerless over everything outside of myself. And yet, in that powerlessness, I found something I never expected: freedom. The old path led to exhaustion and misery, but this new trail, though uneven and unfamiliar, led to inner peace.

A peace I could carry with me even in the mess and hurt, even when life didn't look the way I wished it would. A peace that would allow me to see things more clearly for what they were and to choose a new way to see reality.

The Healing Space

Because my job was so repetitive and easy, I suddenly had hours of space each day to think and process all that was unfolding within me. Tucked away in that little closet, I could listen to podcasts and audiobooks without interruption while I put names and numbers into the computer data forms. The first thing I found was a playlist of old Al-Anon speaker meetings on Spotify. I devoured every single episode, laughing, crying, and healing.

Then I began listening to spiritual books, teachings on all forms of spirituality and emotional healing, and podcasts about mindset, awakening, and recovery. Six or more hours every day, hours that used to be filled with stress and striving, were now filled with wisdom pouring into me as nourishment. My heart and soul were finally ready to receive it.

Something in me began to shift again. I realized how tightly I had been gripping everyone else's life, trying to fix, manage, and reshape what was never mine to hold. In the process, I had forgotten myself. I had forgotten my own purpose, my own healing, my wholeness, and the wholeness of everyone I loved.

Spirit had given me the time and space to breathe, to soften, and to absorb new language and new ways of thinking. To reset my nervous system, to begin to shift my perception, and to deeply heal.

It felt like more and more pieces of the puzzle were clicking into place. Sometimes I think of that season as my time as a sponge that was finally wrung out and emptied of the darkness, control, addiction, and codependency, leaving me receptive to what was to come.

I was no longer dripping with the heaviness of old patterns. I was an open vessel, ready to soak up light. Ready to take in what could restore me, reshape me, and make me new.

I wanted to heal and was willing to do whatever it took to do so. I was dedicated to my meetings, showing up again and again, and in those moments, I truly let go of trying to control everything around me. I turned my attention inward and saw how much of my power I had given away.

I had been living under the belief that if my family members were OK, then I could be OK. But the truth was, I had always been powerless over whether they were OK.

What I began to realize was simple, yet profound: I get to choose if I am going to be OK or even happy. Years earlier, I had made up a quote I used to tell the kids all the time: "You get to choose your attitude. Pick a good one." But I hadn't always been living or modeling it.

Because it's bigger than just choosing your attitude. It's choosing your life. Pick a good one. It's choosing how you're going to show up in the world. Choose a healthy way to see and be in the world.

And oddly enough, it was in that dark closet at that temporary job where this truth landed in me. It was there that I finally had space to fill myself up, to heal my nervous system, and to tend to my own heart. To detox from the complexity of a job I had once loved that had turned toxic, from a family I cherished that had become unmanageable. Not by trying to change them, but by finally learning to accept them.

> *"God, grant me the serenity to accept the things I cannot change, the courage to change the things I can, and the wisdom to know the difference."*

The Transformation

I believe this step of admitting I was powerless and letting go of control was the real turning point. It was where things began to shift, where life started to open up, and where I could finally begin to piece together my own puzzle in a way that felt clearer and more aligned to my Higher Self and authentic way of being.

And the most surprising part? The more I let go of control over my family, the more they began to step into responsibility, both emotionally and practically, for the very things I had carried for them for so long.

Alex and his dad were working out their relationship in their own way. It wasn't how I would have scripted it, but it was theirs to live. Alex was working for Rich and living on his own. Bodhi had gone off to college, and suddenly Rich and I were alone in the house, stepping into life as empty nesters. In all of this, I saw the shift that happens when you get out of the way.

That, I believe, was the beginning of healing for me, for them, and for all of us.

It is so important to allow everyone their own experience. Spiritually, I see now what I couldn't then: I hadn't been able to recognize them as souls on their own journeys. Now I understand that we come here with a deeper soul purpose to learn and grow as we walk through complex, sticky, and sometimes painful experiences. Transformation and growth do not come from an easy ride, they come from challenge and seeing we are so much more than we believe from our small selves.

Life's challenges are the curriculum our souls experience in the school of life. By trying to control my family members' lives, I was blocking their lessons and interfering with the awakening that was meant for them. I was seeing them as broken and lost, when in truth there is nothing wrong with us. We only forget and can get caught in the storm of fear.

Now I see differently. We are here to learn and grow through what feels difficult, to loosen our grip on control and attachment, and to remember the deeper truth, which is that underneath it all we are already whole, more worthy than we have given ourselves permission to believe.

I had been so consumed with trying to manage and fix the people in my life that I couldn't see them in their wholeness. In my striving, I was keeping them from living their own lives and from walking their own soul journeys exactly as they were meant to unfold for their greatest learning and growing, easy and hard.

Letting go of control was the true beginning of my spiritual journey. It was the first real shift, the opening that changed everything. Allowing them their experience and stopping myself from trying to change it, fix it, heal it, or make it different, and instead turning my attention inward, focusing on my own well-being, growth, happiness, freedom, and my own spiritual journey.

This was where the real journey to recover my soul began. **Not the day I put down the drink, but the day I began to put down control.**

Working the Steps in Your Own Life

Recover Your Soul - STEP 2

2. Release Control

Identify Attachments: **Recognize that your pain and suffering come from attachment to control and the illusion of power over external circumstances.** *Embrace Powerlessness:* **Accept that you are powerless over everything outside yourself, and that true strength and peace come from within.**

***

This chapter has been about that turning point when I finally began to loosen my grip and take my power back. For so long, I gave my power away, I believed my peace depended on everything and everyone around me. If I could just manage it all, fix it all, keep it all together, then maybe I would feel safe. What I discovered is that the suffering was not in the people or the problems – it was in my need to control them.

Step 2 of the Recover Your Soul Process invites us to recognize that truth. We identify our attachments and see clearly that our pain comes from the illusion of power over external circumstances. Control is not strength. It's exhausting. And yet, hidden inside that realization is a gift: freedom. When we embrace our powerlessness over everything outside ourselves, we discover that true strength and peace come from within.

Releasing control does not mean we stop caring. It does not mean life stops being messy. It means we learn to let people have their own journeys while we tend to our own. We choose presence over worry, acceptance over anxiety, and trust over manipulation.

True healing begins when we release the exhausting work of managing the unmanageable and allow Spirit to show us another way.

If you feel called to go deeper into this step, I invite you to listen to these Recover Your Soul podcast episodes where I share my own messy, beautiful journey of letting go.

Podcasts About Releasing Control

https://recoveryoursoulbook.com/

CHAPTER 4:
Looking in the Mirror

"Until you make the unconscious conscious, it will direct your life, and you will call it fate." –- Carl Jung

We all carry powerful stories that are woven with joy and shadow, moments of beauty and moments of deep pain. And when we're in the middle of it, it can feel almost impossible to understand why we have to go through this pain, what caused it, and to see what the pain is trying to teach us.

In counseling sessions, our minister used to tell Rich and me that we were together on purpose. Yet through the hardest years, I couldn't understand why our life had to be so complicated. Why did it have to hurt so much? Why did I think and feel the way I did? In my most painful moments, I even questioned why my soul had chosen this life and this husband.

But those questions, instead of being harsh judgments against myself, became the doorway to further light and knowledge. In working the 12 Steps of AA and Al-Anon, my story began to surface in a new way.

Step Four of the 12 Steps asks us to make "a searching and fearless moral inventory of ourselves," and it was here that I began to sit with those deeper questions: What is my part in all of this? Why do I hold these beliefs? What patterns keep repeating in my life? Who am I beneath it all?

And then came the harder invitation: What isn't working? Am I willing to look honestly in the mirror and take responsibility for my own well-being, my own healing, and my own happiness?

If I were truly letting go of control over everything outside myself, would I also be willing to step into my own awakening, to witness and heal my own story, and to allow real change to begin?

The Courage to Change What I Can

I came back again to the Serenity Prayer:

God, grant me the serenity to accept the things I cannot change, the courage to change the things I can….

I was finally understanding that the second line of the Serenity Prayer, which says, "the courage to change the things I can," was about me! I could glimpse the truth that there was nothing wrong with me. For so long, I had carried the belief that I was broken, that everything around me was broken. But what if that wasn't true?

What if our patterns, beliefs, and stories aren't "bad" at all but simply part of our human journey? What if they are not proof of failure but the raw material of growth? If I could come to understand what lived inside my own mind, including the beliefs and stories I had clung to so tightly, then maybe there could be real, lasting change in me.

That is the work of Step Four: making a searching and fearless moral inventory. In both AA and Al-Anon, you're given very specific guidance on how to write this step, how to lay out your resentments and your hurts, and then look honestly at your own part in them. To see, maybe for the first time, how much of what you've been carrying was shaped not only by others but by your own role and your own reactions.

In the recovery community, humility and awareness are at the heart of this step. Addiction, after all, is a profoundly selfish disease, leaving harm and heartbreak in its wake. Humility is essential for healing to begin.

As I did this work, I opened to the spiritual practices that had always been a part of my life but that I had not learned to use. Instead of shame, I chose compassion. Instead of judgment, I offered myself grace. With each belief and pattern revealed, I began to see not brokenness, but the possibility of transformation.

Questioning the Why

Why did I have these beliefs? Why did I think it was my job to take care of everyone else? Why did a part of me feel that I had to over-function, that I had to help and fix, to make things be different, that I thought I knew better? What was actually underneath all those unconscious forces?

As I sat in that temporary job listening to Al-Anon speaker meetings hour after hour on Spotify, I began to hear patterns in my own story that I'd never noticed before. The same themes continued to recur in my journals across decades.

My journal entry for March 12, 2001:

> *I have to take care of myself and everyone else, and I feel like I need and want to be cared for. But here's the rub. I want to be giving Alex and Bodhi the foundation of feeling uncondition-ally loved, and I am, and I'm doing a really crappy job.*

Was I willing to actually open the doors to my memories and stories to understand more about myself? Was I truly willing to look in the mirror with honesty and humility?

One of the gifts of recovery is that the idea of releasing shame becomes normal. There is an invitation to stop judging yourself, to stop giving yourself ultimatums about being perfect or living up to an unrealistic standard. In the rooms of recovery, you begin to discover that healing is possible no matter how far you have fallen.

I would learn much later that perfectionism, meaning my drive to be perfect and take care of everything and everyone, is really just a form of protection and a way of guarding my heart and trying to create safety. As I began to quiet my mind and release the constant need to take care of everyone else, I finally had a moment to reflect on what was actually happening within me.

Going Back to the Beginning

In recovery I recognized that to truly understand myself, I had to look back at my childhood and to the beliefs, stories, and patterns shaped by my younger self. Not from a place of victimhood or complaint, but with compassion and grace for the unique and complex circumstances that had formed me.

Now that my mind was clear in sobriety, now that I was in my late 40s with more life behind me, with years of spiritual exploration and a new perspective of recovery through the 12 Steps, I could see the gift being offered.

The gift was in looking deeply at myself and, through these tools, learning to offer grace, compassion, and understanding for what I had lived through.

It was time to see my life through a new lens. Not the lens that complained endlessly in my journals. Not the lens that replayed therapy session after therapy session, where I groaned about how unfair it all was, how much it hurt. Not even the lens I had used in couples counseling with Rich, where I filled the "safe" space with everything I didn't like about him and about our life together.

This was different. This was a lens that let me understand myself and why my life hurt so much.

I began to see that the patterns I carried were not flaws. Instead, they were born from the beliefs and stories written into me as a child for survival. Those early experiences became the invisible script of my life, teaching me who I thought I had to be in order to feel safe and loved. Beneath it all, my soul had never forgotten the truth of who I was; it waited patiently for me to remember.

Of course they are. Those childhood experiences set the stage for how I would later walk through the world as an adult.

Recognizing the Patterns

It was clear that I was codependent.

It was clear that I was a people-pleaser.

It was clear that I believed it was my job to be the peacemaker.

Looking back on my life, I could see how these patterns had been controlling me for years. But now I wanted to understand how they had become so prominent in the first place and how they shaped the way I was showing up in the world.

As I examined these patterns more closely, though working Step Four in AA, I began to notice the underlying beliefs. The beliefs we carry are often hidden from us because they feel like truth rather than perspective. However, when we approach them with curiosity instead of judgment, we can see how they've been shaping our reality. Through this exploration, I began to see the root of my patterns.

"I'm not enough."

I began to recognize that belief had been with me since childhood. Not smart enough, not pretty enough, not comfortable in my own skin. This discomfort was why I drank and why I tried to control. My journals repeat this refrain for decades. From 2015:

> *I'm fat... old... ugly... stupid... undesirable... I'm a bad wife... a*
> *bad mother... I'm a fraud... I'm not worthy... I'm not enough.*

This unconscious belief of not being enough and fearing rejection drove my people-pleasing, my perfectionism, and my efforts not to disappoint anyone. If I wasn't enough on my own, then I had to find my value through what I could do for others, and it created a set of beliefs in which I viewed everything.

"I have to take care of everyone." This belief made me feel responsible for other people's emotions and outcomes. If someone was unhappy, it was my job to fix it. If there was a conflict, I had to resolve it. If someone was struggling, I had to save them.

"Conflict is dangerous." Growing up in a home with no visible conflict left me completely unprepared for normal human disagreement. Any tension felt like a threat to the entire system.

In 2005, I wrote in my journal:

> *I don't know that you could have conflict and be OK. I thought*
> *we were supposed to avoid conflict at all costs.*

"I'm only as happy as my least happy child." This belief became a prison. I couldn't allow myself joy or peace if any family member was struggling. My own well-being was entangled with theirs, making me emotionally dependent on everyone else's well-being.

How had this become an invisible set of rules to live by? As I began letting go of control, I found more opportunities to look in the mirror and search for myself. I became more and more curious.

What could I learn from being the child of divorced parents, raised by a single mother, feeling like the only space available to me was to be helpful and good? It's no wonder I became the "good little girl." I was highly rewarded for it. I was highly rewarded for being independent and resourceful from a very young age.

In fact, I recently had a conversation with my mom about how intentional she had been in raising me to be independent, strong, capable of taking care of anything, and needing no one. And she succeeded. But that upbringing had left some gaps in how I could allow myself to be loved.

What I see now is that through those experiences, I also formed other beliefs, and one of those was that to be loved, I needed to be self-reliant and good. That it wasn't safe to ask for help. That others' needs always came before mine. That it wasn't safe to let people in.

The Painful Memories

When I looked underneath those feelings, I uncovered painful memories and core wounds. I remembered being a little girl in a neighborhood full of kids, yet always feeling like an outsider. I wasn't liked or included.

As the only child of a single mom who was now working and supporting us, I was pushed into other families' homes after school or when she went out of town for work, and I knew I wasn't really wanted there. Kids can be cruel, and I mostly felt like I was on the outside looking in.

I remember being rejected by the other girls at my elementary school, never being able to meet the qualifications to join their "clubs," and how deeply painful that was. I remember the lonely existence of playing by myself, wondering what was wrong with me. We did not have much, and my mom always made sure I had what I needed, but we rarely had enough for me to have what I wanted.

So I learned not only not to ask but also not to want. As it was just my mom and me, I was treated more like an adult from a very young age, and there wasn't much room for my childhood. My mother loved me very much; however, her life was the center of everything we did, and I was just along for the ride.

From that, I was rewarded for my independence, strong will, and ability to go with the flow of our life without complaints or desires. My mother was quiet and peaceful, and there was more silence than conversation and never conflict. Even early on between my parents, there was never conflict. I did not break the rules or even push the boundaries because I learned early to be a people-pleaser and the importance of my role as a peacemaker.

As I dug deeper into these childhood memories, into questions pertaining to how to be accepted, how to be loved, how to show up in the world, what lay beneath my codependency, and what fueled that part of me that didn't trust anyone, that believed I had to take care of everything because I wasn't safe, a profound memory emerged.

The Core Wound: The Christmas Secret

I have a memory from Christmas, just before my fourth birthday. My mother was sewing a shirt for my father on an old-fashioned sewing machine, the kind with a foot pedal she pushed back and forth as she carefully guided the fabric.

I watched with fascination as she worked, creating a beautiful velvet New Mexican shirt with silver buttons. She told me it was a secret, that I mustn't tell anyone because it was going to be my father's Christmas surprise. But I didn't understand what secrets were. I didn't know what it meant to keep information from someone, because I had always been so open and honest.

Of course, before Christmas came, I told him.

That particular memory belongs to a little girl who had never really gotten in trouble. A little girl who had already learned to just be good, to say yes, to do the right thing, to play by herself, to be quiet, and to be the "good little girl." And yet, in this situation, I got into a lot of trouble.

In my memory, I was yelled at and spanked. I remember being put outside, standing on the front porch, crying at the closed door, afraid. As an adult, I can look back and imagine that my front porch was probably a safe place to be. Maybe my parents put me outside because the house was small and they were having their own argument and wanted to keep it from me. Maybe they thought they were protecting me from it. I had never seen or heard them argue.

But what I remember clearly is that they were both angry, and not just at me, but at each other.

What I've discovered in recovering my soul is this: The feelings and memories I carry are uniquely my own, and they matter. **Often, we dismiss our own feelings and memories because we view them through the lens of our adult selves or the desire to protect the others in the story.**

We understand more now, and we can put things into perspective. But in doing so, we don't actually allow ourselves to feel those moments as the child we once were.

The Decision That Changed Everything

As I was processing this inner child work and accessing this core wound, what I realized is that I had never really been in trouble before, and that this particular experience was so profoundly painful for me that I made a decision right then and there to never be in trouble again. That if I ever did something like that again, it meant that love would be removed from me.

These core wounds are the foundation of our beliefs and operating system in the world, and in that moment, fear and pain created a protective system to keep me safe. The solution to my safety was to never get in trouble again and to keep everyone happy.

"If I'm good enough, nothing bad will happen."

This magical thinking stemmed from this core wound at age 3 when I got in trouble for revealing my mom's surprise. That little girl decided that bad things happen when you're not careful enough, good enough, or quiet enough.

When I was able to unpack this as an adult and see the amount of pain sustained by this core wound, it began to release the power it had held deep in my subconscious.

We all have core wounds and stories that come from our younger selves. I recognize now how profoundly it affected every aspect of my life. How I made every decision after that based on this particular memory of safety, of being enough, of doing the right thing, and of never getting in trouble. This was the beginning of truly looking in the mirror.

It's not about blaming somebody else; it's not about judging my parents as good or bad. I think the beauty of what I've learned through what I now call Recover Your Soul is that there's no judgment. Each situation is what it is, and each person shows up with the best they have at that moment, which often is hurtful to another person. **Recovering your soul begins when we look within, not to judge, but to understand ourselves with love and grace.**

One Thanksgiving, the revealed secret story came up somehow, and my dad quickly dismissed it, saying that was not how he remembered it at all. And that's OK. We don't have to justify how we feel. We don't have to justify our memories. They don't have to be the same memories that somebody else has because the only thing that really matters is how they were to us. Everything is neutral, but we each have our own unique experience of it, and it is essential that we are given the space to have our own perception.

Big Traumas and Daily Patterns

As I kept looking at my patterns and the stories that shaped me, I began to see something I hadn't seen before. The Christmas shirt moment was a big "T" trauma for me and a wound that made an imprint on my sense of safety and belonging. But so much of who I became didn't come from dramatic moments. It came from the quieter places. The daily rhythms. The unspoken dynamics. The ways I learned to make sense of the world as a sensitive little girl and only child.

When I was born, my parents were living in a simple house far outside Santa Fe where there was no running water and no electricity. It wasn't a hardship; it was the life they wanted and what had drawn them to New Mexico in the first place. My mother loved those early years with me out in the quiet. My father worked in town at the guitar shop and played music with his band, which meant he wasn't home much.

That was simply our life. Even after we eventually moved into Santa Fe, the pattern stayed the same: my mom working odd jobs, doing the best she could, and my dad mostly absent, following his own passions.

Our life was simple. I know we had what we needed, but from a very young age I felt the sense that we didn't have much. I learned very early not to ask for anything, not to want too much, and to be good and easy.

I have memories of my parents laughing more when I was very young, but when I look back through old photographs, I notice something striking: my mother is never smiling in the pictures. Even before I understood it, something wasn't working for them. They still loved one another and still respected one another, but their lives no longer fit together. When my mom came back from India when I was eight, they made the loving decision to separate. The truth was that my dad hadn't really lived with us for a while by then.

I was a little girl who desperately wanted her father's attention and affection, and that longing became a defining thread in my life. Later, it became the foundation of my pattern of seeking men's approval and trying to shape myself into whoever I thought they wanted me to be, while losing myself in the process and forming my codependent behaviors.

Another layer of my childhood that I didn't understand until much later was the quiet but constant presence of marijuana when I was growing up. My dad smoked regularly, not in a chaotic or dramatic way, but as a steady companion woven into the rhythm of his life. No one called it addiction. It was simply normal, much like families where a nightly drink is just part of the routine. But "normal" does not mean neutral. Even the most socially accepted forms of checking out shape the emotional world a child grows up in.

I have often told the story of being a little girl handing out joints on a tray at parties much like someone would glasses of wine. I loved being part of the fun of the adults and have memories of sneaking off with leftover joints and taking a few drags, likely when I was in elementary school with the other kids.

I can see now how these subtle patterns affected me. There was a tenderness and a sweetness in my dad, but there was also a distance, the kind that comes from being under the influence of anything. As a little girl who longed for closeness with her father, I absorbed the message that the adults around me needed something outside themselves to relax or be at ease.

Without realizing it, I was already learning the early stories of codependence, escape, and self-abandonment that I would later act out in my own ways.

By my early twenties, I turned to marijuana the way he had because it felt familiar, like a learned rhythm for softening the edges of my world. These are the quieter inheritances that shape us. They don't look like a "problem," yet they carve grooves in our beliefs about who we are, what we deserve, and how we cope. This is where Step 3 begins, in telling the truth about the stories we absorbed long before we had words for them.

My mom, strong and fiercely independent, returned to her dream of working in science after India. She went back to school, all the way through her Ph.D. in chemistry. She did what she needed to do in order to make her life what she wanted. I admire her so much for that. And at the same time, those years added another layer to my belief system that other people's needs came first and that I was there to support, adapt, and stay out of the way. My inner belief was that being "good" was the safest place I could be.

I became a latchkey kid in late elementary school. TV became my companion. Money was tight. New clothes came maybe twice a year. I always felt like I didn't have what the other kids had. I carried that sense of "not enough" into adulthood with a fear around money and a belief that there would never be enough for me.

When I finally examined this through the lens of healing, I understood why I overbought groceries as an adult and why thrift stores became my treasure hunt. I was trying to soothe the little girl inside me, the one who wanted to feel cared for, provided for, and abundant.

None of this came from addiction or dramatic dysfunction. It came from being a sensitive child trying to make sense of her world. It came from longing for attention, learning independence too young, and believing that being helpful and quiet made me safe. That other's needs were more important than mine, and if I needed or wanted anything, I had to get it for myself.

I had once said with pride that I started working at 13 and never stopped, but now I could see that it was something I had to do and not something that I wanted to do.

And as I began to see this clearly, not with blame or judgement, but with compassion - I felt something soften inside me. I could hold the grief of the lonely child I was and the tenderness of the strong woman I was becoming. I could see that my parents loved me fiercely and still didn't have the tools to show up in the ways my sensitive little heart needed. None of it was wrong. None of it was their fault. It was simply the landscape I learned to navigate.

And this is the heart of the process: the moment we stop judging the past and begin to understand it. The moment we align with a new perception rooted in compassion, clarity, and truth. **This is where recovering your soul begins: in the willingness to see yourself clearly, to honor the child you once were, and to remember that you now have the power to choose a new path and a new way to see it.**

Building the Belief System

All those times that I was ridiculed and teased by other children, all those times that I felt like I wasn't enough, were building a belief system in me. I was put in elementary school classes for remedial students. I felt I was being told on a regular basis that I wasn't that smart in a million little ways.

My subconscious was looking for evidence of how I was not enough, and so I was given cues and information on a regular basis that indicated something wrong with me, and I began to believe it.

Of course, I was building up a belief system that validated this as my truth of who I was and helped create the patterns that would play out in my life.

I wouldn't challenge myself for fear that I would be seen as not being that smart. I repeated this all the time, self-deprecating comments about not being good enough or smart enough. Now I see how that played into my job of trying so desperately to prove myself and get some sort of validation. The reason I held on so tightly to control in my job as the office manager was because it was a position where I felt smart and validated.

It was essential that I felt recognized and valued, and I could begin to dismantle the belief system of a little girl who had said, "You're not enough." But every time I would potentially get into trouble, if my children would get in trouble, or if there was conflict in my home, I didn't recognize that it was a little girl who was afraid of being in trouble that would do anything, and I mean anything, to not feel those feelings.

We all have experiences as children, big and small, that shape how we see ourselves and our world, and we try to explain what we feel, especially when we are having big feelings that our little bodies cannot understand or process.

Understanding the Origins

I was beginning to understand the foundations that created my codependent behaviors. Losing myself for fear of getting in trouble has played into every aspect of my life. I began to recognize, through my exploration of this aspect of myself, that examining my own shadow without judgment or blame, but rather with curiosity, is the beginning of deep and profound healing.

Beyond individual beliefs were the larger stories I'd constructed about my life, my family, and my role in the world:

"I'm the victim of other people's addictions and dysfunction."

This story cast me as the long-suffering saint trying to hold everything together while surrounded by difficult people. Reading through my journals, I could see this victim narrative clearly when I wrote:

> *I'm only getting older and older and letting my life slip by. Is there happiness in this relationship? I don't really like to be around Rich because he's generally intense, bossy, frustrated, or hyper or overly physical.*

"I'm responsible for fixing what's broken in my family."

This story made me the center of everyone's healing journey. From my journal during Alex's struggles:

> *My entire world has revolved around Alex and how to help him for almost five years. In those years, I've held on so tightly to the outcome I wanted.*

That little girl was activated whenever my husband was upset, whenever my children were upset. My fear of not doing the right thing had been the foundation that set up every pattern and every way I showed up.

I wanted to fix it so badly so that I wouldn't be in trouble, so that I would be safe, so that I would be OK. If they were OK, then I could be OK. Under that need for them to be OK was a need for me to be loved. My subconscious was terrified of rejection.

This marked the beginning of a healing journey, during which I began to realize that this wasn't about the people in my life. It wasn't about how someone else felt. It wasn't about how someone else interpreted the story. I began to recognize the value and importance of what I saw and felt for myself.

What if it's not about trying to change them but about what's happening in me? How can I be more compassionate to myself? How can I open myself up to understand where the stories, patterns, and beliefs came from?

Once I began to truly examine how much my life had been shaped by my childhood and adolescent experiences, I recognized that it was the little 4-year-old girl who stood in the living room or kitchen when so much was happening in my adult life.

When my husband and kids were fighting, my little girl didn't know how to handle it. Of course she didn't. She was just a little girl. She didn't know how to handle it when she was 4, and she didn't know how to handle it as a young woman or even as an adult.

Remembering the Teachings

Then I began to remember and to take in all the information I had gathered over the years through my spiritual teachings and practices. I recalled a class at my church about the wounded child, and suddenly it was as if all the puzzle pieces from a lifetime of study began to fall into place.

I remembered learning how we carry these core memories and how the inner child feels hurt, sad, and wounded, and how the stories they create are simply attempts to make sense of what they cannot understand. As soon as I brought those teachings back into awareness, new opportunities to deepen my healing began to flow into my life.

It was as if a door had opened, inviting me to explore inner child work more fully, to look at my core wounds, and to see how the systems I had built shaped the way I showed up in the world. And with that awareness, I could finally offer myself grace. I could begin to say, "Of course I felt overwhelmed. Of course I was trying to control my very complicated and painful life."

There truly had been very difficult things happening in my family, and now I was beginning to understand why I reacted the way I did and why I saw it the way I did.

I didn't grow up in a childhood with fighting or conflict. In my home, the rule was simple: you didn't say or do anything that might create it conflict. Above all, keep things peaceful. My mom only had to say she was disappointed, and that was one of the worst things I could imagine.

I saw my dad lose his temper only a handful of times, and it was never with me. It was with his second wife and his stepson. I had developed an intense need to make sure I was never in trouble and to make sure no one else was either. That, to me, was what felt safe.

From my journal in 2009, *I could see the pattern clearly:*

I was the daughter of an independent child. I was the only child of a single mother. She was a wonderful mother, but she modeled for me at a very young age to be a good little girl, to not rock any boats, to be independent, and to be self-sufficient. And that gave me the belief that it was my job to take care of everybody else.

Getting Honest Feedback

When things were falling apart at my office manager job, I went to lunch with a woman I deeply respected, someone who had done extensive consulting for the company. I was at the start of my sobriety journey, hungry for honest feedback, and I asked her what blind spots she saw in me and how I could improve as I prepared to move on to a new job.

Her response was immediate: she told me I could be self-righteous and that my blind spot was jumping in too quickly to try to fix things without first stepping back to see the bigger picture. As painful and difficult as it was to hear, she was right.

That conversation became a turning point. I became more determined than ever to understand the unhealthy side of that tendency and to learn how to stand on the healthy side of who I was. I take pride in being well-organized, having good ideas, and being able to get things done. But I needed to separate those strengths from the self-righteous belief that I knew the best way.

Looking at Character Defects

Part of the 12 Steps is examining what AA calls character defects, and this practice became central to my healing. Working with a sponsor in Step Five, I began using this tool to understand myself more honestly and to witness the early signs of transformation. It helped me see that I could choose—moment by moment—whether to show up from love or from fear.

As I worked through this process, it felt like holding up a mirror. I was doing the shadow work, uncovering the patterns, beliefs, and stories that had shaped how I viewed the world and how I moved through it. What emerged was the realization that this work wasn't only about awareness; it was about responsibility.

I began owning the ways I had shown up that no longer served me, the people around me, or the situations I found myself in.

The Steps of Accountability

I was in the process of looking at this pattern when I began working with my sponsor on Step Five and what AA calls "character defects." In the traditional 12-Step process, after completing your fearless moral inventory in Step Four, you move on to Step Five, which is admitting to God, to yourself, and to another human being the exact nature of your wrongs. Then Step Six asks you to become entirely ready to have God remove those defects.

But working those steps with my sponsor wasn't just about filling in a worksheet. It was standing face-to-face with the way I saw the world, the defenses I had built to survive, and the choice of whether I was going to keep living from those old patterns of fear or find a healthier way.

As we went deeper, I began to recognize that my familiar "go-to" reactions, or what the program called defects, were really defense mechanisms. They were born from my subconscious beliefs, childhood wounds, and a desperate need to protect myself.

I don't use the language of "defect" anymore. To me, these were not flaws so much as protectors or strategies my younger self created to stay safe. Of course, I set up systems to cope. Of course, I reached for control, judgment, and over-functioning. Those defenses made sense and even worked at times in my life.

What became clear, though, was the cost. The very patterns that once had kept me safe had caused pain and conflict in my family. And with compassion for myself, I could finally see and admit that I had played a part in the dysfunction of our complicated relationships.

My List of Defenses

As I sat in silence after hours of sharing Step Five, my own list became painfully clear. These were the patterns I ran to when I felt unsafe:

Withdrawal. Self-seeking. Victimhood and self-pity. Self-righteousness. Fear and avoidance. Controlling tendencies (oh yes!). Defensiveness. Denial. Enabling behavior. Judgment. Gossip. Anxiety. Isolation. Closing myself off. Selfishness.

I began to see that I did, in fact, have a choice in how I responded. These patterns weren't who I truly was. They were survival tools I reached for when I was hurting.

When my heart was broken, when life didn't show up the way I needed it to, when I was scared or out of control, this is how I reacted. I withdrew. I tried to manage. I judged. I defended. I over-functioned. I controlled.

This was the woman Rich saw when I was in pain. It wasn't my authentic self, but my wounded self, fighting at every turn, trying to bend our lives into what I believed would make us OK. Even though I thought I was acting from love, those defenses were causing harm.

Looking in the mirror, I realized the only thing I could change was me. By naming these defenses with honesty, I could finally see my pain for what it was – fear – and could begin to release it.

> **From my journal in 2010,** *I was finally ready to ask the hard questions:*
>
> *What is my part, Rachel? Where have you been showing up in this? Who are you in this? What is your responsibility?*

Later, as my spiritual journey deepened and I learned more about psychology and healing, I came to understand that these patterns were not flaws at all but protectors standing guard at the door of my pain. They were the defense mechanisms my psyche had built to try to keep me safe. And with that awareness, I began to appreciate them. I began to see them with grace and gratitude for what they had done for me.

Over time, I could recognize that these parts of myself had served an important purpose. They helped me survive. But I had reached a place where I no longer needed them, and I no longer wanted to rely on those particular tools.

Still, it was vital to honor them. To offer kindness, compassion, and gratitude to every part of my shadow self, for it had only ever been doing the best it could with what it knew and what it had learned up until then.

A Place of Compassion, Not Judgment

This was also the person who hadn't been easy to work with in the office manager job. This was the part of me that believed she had the right answer to everything, the part that was quick to be self-righteous and certain.

But now I could see that underneath it all, it was about protection. For the first time, I understood this wasn't a place for judgment, but a place to offer kindness and compassion to myself. My Higher Self was beginning to come online, guiding me toward healing and helping me release the shame of my small, fearful self.

I felt grateful for all the spiritual lessons and tools I had been gathering over the years. Even when I didn't fully understand how to apply the principles from Sunday talks, book studies, or the songs we sang, they had been a lifeline, keeping my head above water in the years of struggle. Thank goodness I had been part of a spiritual community that taught God as love, not judgment.

It was as if those teachings were finally coming into focus, as if I was truly beginning to awaken.

I was beginning to believe there was nothing wrong with me. These old defenses I had relied on for so long were simply no longer the solution. I could see them for what they were: coping tools that had helped me survive. But I didn't want to keep living through them.

That was when Step Six spoke to me with new meaning: **We're entirely ready to have God remove all these character defects.**

I didn't hear it as condemnation anymore. I heard it as an invitation. An opening to let Spirit lift the weight, to release the defenses and step fully into the light of grace.

I recognized that I had choices and more choices than I ever believed I had. The more I let go of control, the more I released the need to fix and manage everything around me, and the more freedom I felt to live in a new way. And I began to wonder: What would it be like to lay down these old tools completely? What if I no longer needed them at all?

The Operating System Analogy

We are constantly updating, learning, expanding, and changing. I often use the analogy of computers to explain our beliefs as an operating system. If you are working on a PC and your Word document stops working, you press control plus alt and delete, the task manager comes up, and you reset the program. But underneath all of that, there is still the box of code, the operating system, that runs the programs.

Most of us do not realize that we are still running on operating systems that have never been updated.

Some are corrupted or missing important code. They are built from the beliefs, stories, and patterns of our younger selves, created in fear, created with limited understanding of the world. And when the programs stop working, including our relationships, jobs, and interactions, it is often a sign that the operating system itself is outdated.

I was running on an operating system that said, "Never get in trouble. To be loved, you must behave a certain way. You must take care of everything. If you do anything wrong, you will be abandoned, and you will be rejected."

That operating system does not work, and it is not true.

So even though I could reset the "programs," such as my relationships and circumstances, if I did not change what was underneath, if I did not change that subconscious belief system within myself, then my patterns could never truly change.

Coming Home to Myself

By looking at these beliefs and stories, I began to see that this was never about being unworthy or broken. It was about understanding myself with compassion. My wounds weren't proof that something was wrong with me; they were invitations to come home, to remember my whole-ness, to reconnect with the soul that had been there all along.

I realized I could choose how I showed up. I could choose how I saw the world. My perceptions weren't fixed and they could shift. Even the painful experiences carried value; they had shaped me, and now they could teach me. I was ready to stop living as a victim, to stand in emp-owerment, and to align my life with my Higher Self and the purpose of my soul.

Now, when I notice myself wanting to withdraw, or when fear, defen-siveness, or anxiety rise up, I see it as information. Instead of condem-ning myself, I can pause and ask: What is this really showing me? What is this part of me trying to protect? Each trigger became a teacher.

As I practiced this, life began to change. When the buttons were pushed, I had the power to pause and look within rather than trying to control someone else. And in that space of surrender, Spirit met me.

The beauty was that as I released my grip and trusted what I call Spirit – Source, God, the Universe – the doors opened on their own. The puzzle pieces began to fall into place. At home, things softened. Within myself, I felt lighter. The next steps revealed themselves, one after another, without me forcing or fixing.

All I needed was the willingness to let go. To flow with life. To release my attachment to the old patterns and stories and to stay curious about what might be waiting just beyond the next breath.

Looking in the mirror no longer felt like an act of self-criticism. It became an act of self-love. Every pattern carried a story, and every story held a key to my healing. **The courage to change the things I could was guiding me back to myself.**

This was the beginning of freedom. Not only freedom from substan-ces, but freedom from the unconscious programming that had once made substances feel necessary at all.

Working the Steps in Your Own Life

Recover Your Soul - STEP 3

3. Discover Unhealthy Patterns, Beliefs, and Stories
Examine Patterns, Beliefs, and Stories: **Identify and acknowledge the unhealthy patterns, beliefs, and stories; often formed in childhood and shaped by family, culture, and conditioning that have influenced your life and behavior.** *Recognize Their Impact:* **Understand how these unconscious patterns have created suffering and shaped your perception of self, others, and the world.**

***

This chapter has been about discovery and pulling back the curtain on the protective and unhealthy beliefs, patterns, and stories that shaped the way I saw myself and the world around me. For so long, I lived unaware of these subconscious beliefs that kept me in patterns of codependency and people-pleasing. I did not understand that they were simply survival strategies, tools of a younger self who did the best she could with what she knew at the time.

Step 3 of the Recover Your Soul Process invites us to examine the patterns, beliefs, and stories, often formed in childhood and shaped by family, culture, and conditioning, that have influenced our lives. We begin to understand that these unconscious programs have created suffering and shaped our perception of ourselves, others, and the world.

My wounds weren't signs of brokenness. They were invitations to learn, grow, and live from my soul's journey and wholeness.

The courage to face these truths allowed me to see that I had a choice. **I could keep repeating the old stories, or I could release them with compassion and curiosity.**

By recognizing their impact, I could finally stop trying to control everything outside of me and begin to heal and love what was within me.

Step 3 was the beginning of freedom, not only freedom from substances, but freedom from the outdated programming that had made substances and control feel necessary in the first place.

If you feel called to go deeper into discovering your patterns, beliefs, and stories, I invite you to listen to these Recover Your Soul podcast episodes about discovering unhealthy patterns, beliefs, and stories.

Podcasts About Discovering Unhealthy Patterns, Beliefs, and Stories

https://recoveryoursoulbook.com/

C H A P T E R   5 :

Opening to Something Greater Still

The Universe had been speaking all along. I just needed
to be quiet enough to hear. - RH

Even though I had been raised by a Buddhist mother and gone to a Unity Church for over 20 years, the process of healing and awakening to my full self was more of a process than a destination. I had heard the concepts, but I hadn't taken them into my heart and actually learned how to trust and use them until I had hit the wall of my own addiction. It was only when my life had become so complicated and full of pain that I was willing to truly surrender to a spiritual path.

I believe those practices that I had been immersed in had kept my head above water enough to keep me from completely drowning and falling even deeper into despair. If I had not had this constant in my life, I could have fallen even deeper into addiction and destructive choices.

It wasn't until the 12 Steps, when I got on my knees with my sponsor under a tree next to a creek, saying an incredibly powerful Step Three prayer in a ritual of surrender to turn it over... that I felt the shift. With my knees pressed into the earth, the sound of water moving beside me, and the steady presence of someone who had walked this path before, it all came together like a sacred moment carved out of time.

I could feel that surrender wasn't just a word I had heard in sermons or read in books. It was a release, a loosening, a letting go of the grip I had on my own chaos.

I remember the words catching in my throat as tears slid down my face. It wasn't pretty. It wasn't polished. But it was real. In that moment, I stopped carrying the lie that I had to do it all alone. I stopped pretending I was in control. And what came rushing in was the smallest flicker of peace, enough to keep me moving forward, enough to show me there was a path beyond the pain.

"God, I offer myself to Thee to build with me and to do with me as Thou wilt. Relieve me of the bondage of self, that I may better do Thy will. Take away my difficulties, that victory over them may bear witness to those I would help of Thy Power, Thy Love, and Thy Way of Life."

From my journal in 2009 during my first round with sobriety, I had written:

> *God, I am ready. I am ready to change, I am ready to heal, I*
> *am ready to surrender.*

I realized that recovery was not about reaching some grand spiritual mountaintop all at once. It was about showing up in small ways, day after day, with a willingness I had not had before. The willingness to pray even when I did not feel like it. The willingness to sit quietly instead of numbing myself. The willingness to let someone else guide me when my instinct was to take control. What if the will of my Higher Power was for me to be even more than I had allowed myself to believe I deserved?

In those simple practices, I found a new strength. A strength not rooted in control or perfection, but in surrender and trust. What once seemed impossible, or too fragile to risk believing in, became the very ground I stood on.

Each time I let go, even just a little, life seemed to meet me with another gift. A conversation I needed. A moment of laughter when I thought I had forgotten how. An opportunity that made no sense except as grace. These were not coincidences; they were whispers from Spirit.

They were reminders that I was being carried, that I was not alone, and that true soul recovery was not only about surviving. It was about awakening to life itself.

Divine Synchronicity

In January of 2020, my husband and I were watching a Netflix show about authentic tacos. Each episode showed stories and videos of incredible tacos from all over Mexico, and we found ourselves dreaming aloud about how fun it would be to travel there and taste them for ourselves.

Not even a week later, a dear friend of mine called. She worked for a family who had a beach house in Mexico and needed a dog sitter. Would we be interested in being paid to go to Mexico for a week and take care of their dog?

We looked at each other and laughed. Of course we wanted to go! Soon, we were staying at an incredible beach house right on the water, with a Jeep at our disposal and everything we needed to drive into town and eat those delicious, authentic tacos we had just been watching on TV.

It was sitting at that table, surrounded by music and warm air, eating tacos that looked exactly like they had on the show, that I felt the whisper of something greater. The AA Step Three Prayer of opening to co-creation, handing myself over, and letting go of control suddenly became more than just words.

This trip was a living reminder that life could unfold with a grace far beyond what I could orchestrate.

I had spent so much of my life gripping tightly, trying to manage and orchestrate outcomes. And yet here I was, in another country, eating tacos I'd just dreamed about weeks before, because I had been willing to release control and say yes to what Spirit was offering. In that moment, I began to trust more deeply that surrender and co-creation could lead me to a happy and healthy life.

Spiritual Life as Priority

As a spiritual student and lifelong seeker, I began to understand that my spiritual life needed to be my number one priority. For so long, I had made my family my entire focus, trying to fix them, change them, and save them. I had overcompensated for my wounds and fears, constantly trying to prove that I was smart enough, worthy enough, lovable enough, simply... enough.

In the process, I had forgotten that my true work was not out there in the world; it was within me. My spiritual journey had to come first, and I could hand my family over to my Higher Power.

By the end of 2019, six months had passed, and my temporary job was coming to an end. I had spent those months working in my closet office doing data entry, but all the while taking in hundreds of hours of books, podcasts, affirmations, and new loving ideas. That season of quiet learning had already transformed me.

Then I learned about a new job opening at the church I had attended for almost 20 years. It was a part-time position as director of community care. The idea felt like divine order: I could serve in the very community where I had sung, prayed, and grown, and I could utilize the skills I had gathered over the years in a meaningful way.

Yet I found myself in a new place. For perhaps the first time, I did not want to control the outcome. I did not want to force this into being. I wanted it only if it was truly right, not just for me, but also for the church.

When I went in for my interview with two ministers I knew well, one of them the very minister who had supported and counseled my husband and me through all those difficult years, I felt at ease. There was a deep sense of knowing that "this or something better still" was what I was inviting into my life. I was beginning to trust that faith was safe for me.

Most of all, I wanted what was truly right for this community that had meant so much to me for so many years. And as it turned out, the right choice was me. Just as one job was ending, I was able to gently step into the next chapter of my life, a place that felt right and true, where I was fully surrounded by spirituality.

The Power of Visioning

In January 2019, I took a Prosperity Plus class at my spiritual center. It was offered every year, and over the past 20 years, I had taken it numerous times. The teachings were based on spiritual laws, using the principles of the law of attraction to visualize and manifest the life of your dreams.

Part of the Prosperity Plus process was to use a tool that helped clarify vision and goals. The tool divided life into four quadrants: career, relationships, health and time, and money freedom. Once you had clarity, you would write out a full vision of the life you wanted to manifest, then read that vision every day while beginning to take real steps toward it.

The practice was to write as if those dreams and visions were already present, to speak them into existence in detail and with conviction. At that time, I was only a year into sobriety, and there were still many complicated and painful things happening in my life.

I was just beginning to use spiritual principles and 12-Step tools, slowly releasing the need to control and fix my family and working on accepting life as it was. But I had made a decision to embrace healing fully and to step wholeheartedly into whatever processes were offered to me, because I was ready to change the only things I could: myself and my perceptions.

So I drew out my four quadrants and allowed myself to dream, perhaps fully and deeply for the first time. And from that place, I created this vision:

> *I love eating healthy food and being fit, vibrant, and healthy. I am so grateful to have a partner who is my best friend as we enjoy our time together, both at home and as we travel.*
>
> *Our family enjoys spending time together with laughter, love, and pure joy. I love watching the boys live prosperous and independent lives as they follow their passions and dreams. I love spending quality time with my friends.*

I am so grateful to be working in a spiritual field, helping people and inspiring them to live their fullest lives and heal their hearts. My income continues to grow as I work less and our investments increase and prosper and there's zero due on our credit accounts as they are paid in full!

It is a true blessing to be enjoying the beach in the winter and summers in Colorado. I love spending my free time creating music, singing, and making art. This or something better still.

Looking at this now, over six years later, where almost everything I wrote has come into my life, it feels almost unbelievable. At the time, it felt strange to write because nearly all of it was not yet true. My health was shaky, my marriage was unsteady, and my boys were still struggling. I had no idea where my career was headed or how working in a spiritual field could possibly fit. We were drowning in debt, and even the idea of going to the beach in the winter felt like too much to ask.

Still, I was committed to the process. I did everything that was suggested in the class. In the middle of that class is where the temp job had materialized out of what felt like thin air. It was not what was on my vision list, but I kept reading my vision every day and trusting the process. I was opening up to the surrender of allowing the Universe to determine the timing, and by letting go of control, I was willing to just take one small step at a time.

Another miracle. Another moment that reminded me that if I opened my eyes just enough, I could see I had been held and supported all along, even when I could not see it clearly at the time.

An entry from my journal, reflecting on these synchronicities in February of 2019:

That was another God moment. That was another moment where God did for me what I couldn't do for myself... everything in that company blew up. Every relationship blew up. There were meetings that did not go well. There were misunderstandings there, clear markers that this was a solid no, a very solid no. This was the trusting and allowing Spirit, my Higher Power, to guide the way.

Unity and the 12 Steps

While attending a new members' class as a new staff member, I watched a video I had never seen that opened my eyes to something I had never realized before. I learned that AA and Unity, the church I had attended for so many years, were both influenced by similar spiritual foundations that were emerging at that time. There was a deep metaphysical connection between the Big Book of AA and the Unity principles I had been studying. The five basic Unity principles are

1. **God is Absolute Good, present everywhere.** This principle highlights God as the fundamental source and creative power of the Universe, a force that is inherently good and permeates all existence.

2. **Humans are spiritual beings, inherently good.** We are seen as possessing a spark of divinity, or the Christ Spirit, making our core essence divine and therefore good.

3. **Thoughts are creative, shaping our experiences.** Our thinking and beliefs have the power to attract and manifest specific experiences, meaning we are the co-creators of our reality.

4. **Prayer and meditation connect us to the Divine.** Through these practices, we align our consciousness with God, increasing our awareness and bringing forth wisdom, healing, and good into our lives.

5. **We must live the truth we know.** Understanding these spiritual principles is not sufficient; we must actively apply them in our lives through daily actions and inspired living.

I began to see the similarities and understand them in ways that brought me greater awareness and peace. Everything I had heard through the Unity Church, everything I was learning in the AA program, and even my Buddhist background was opening up in new ways.

For the first time, I was truly taking these teachings into my heart and trusting that I could let go.

The Step Three prayer, which I had once recited on my knees by a creek with my sponsor, now spoke to me differently. When I first got sober, I had resisted surrender because I thought it meant giving myself over to the will of a God that I feared. Now I could hear it through the lens of Unity New Thought and metaphysics, which spoke of co-creation.

"God, I offer myself to you to build with me and to do with me as you will."

I could now understand those words as an invitation to come willingly, to go with purpose, humility, and grace. **It was about showing up authentically and building together, not about handing myself over to a distant authority in a subservient way.**

It was seeing that the will of Source was for me to be my fullest and most healed self and recognizing my inherent worthiness. This was a depth of spirituality that had been there all along, but until now, I had not been able to hear or feel it.

Healing Religious Trauma

Back then, I was not ready to let go of control to the will of something I did not yet understand. When I heard the word God, or phrases like "the will of God," it reminded me of the fearful God my grandmother spoke of. Out of her best desire to save my soul, she caused me deep religious trauma by telling me that if I did not believe in God exactly as she did, I would go to hell and that what my parents were teaching me was evil.

I mentioned earlier I was 8 years old when my mom went to India to study with her Buddhist teacher, and I was sent to stay with my grandmother for a month. She spent the entire time trying to save my soul, and it was terrifying.

I came away believing that the God she loved so much required me to be small, subservient, and afraid. And although outwardly I had done all she asked in that month, inside I rejected that God. It did not feel right to me.

I had been raised Buddhist and around incredibly kind and peaceful monks in saffron robes. I remember the scent of sandalwood and the sight of their prayer beads slipping through their fingers as they recited the "Om Mani Padme Hum" mantra in a low, steady chant. There was something profoundly peaceful in the incense and the rhythm of their voices. That was where I felt safe. That was where I felt loved. That was where I first connected with the spiritual world and the idea of a Universal Creator.

My rejection of the word "God" had been so strong that I later realized I was also rejecting the love that could be found there. There are countless words we can use and countless ways to speak of the same thing. **There are many roads that lead to the top of the mountain, and at the summit, it is all the same: love and connection to something Greater Still. A discovery that we are not separate from but one with the energy that has created it all.**

This is one of the things I loved about the Big Book, and it was also what I loved about Unity. No one was telling me who God had to be or exactly what I had to believe. I was being given the freedom to choose for myself, to define the Higher Power of my own understanding.

Some people get caught up in the idea that the 12-Step program is religious, but I do not believe that was its intention. It is spiritual. Step 12 says, "Having had a spiritual awakening as the result of these steps..."

A Deeper Understanding

I was having a spiritual awakening. My heart was beginning to thaw. Feelings that I had long buried were surfacing, and I was starting to see beyond the rigid, closed perception that had been holding everything so tightly together. AA's Step Three Prayer was becoming more and more alive for me, more aligned as a metaphysical prayer.

The next line says, "Relieve me of the bondage of self, that I may better do Your will." From a metaphysical perspective, this is about letting go of our limiting beliefs and fears. It is about recognizing our wholeness and unlimited nature. It is about stepping into our Higher Selves, living fully as the amazing creations we are meant to be.

I had been keeping myself small. I had been afraid to live as my full self. I did not think I knew who I was because I had been living inside old beliefs, the ones that told me I would be rejected and that I didn't know how to be loved.

That fear was still the little girl inside me, the one who was afraid of getting in trouble, of being put outside, of not being chosen to play. It was the part of me that thought if I did not conform or if I was not the wife I believed my husband wanted or the perfect mom I thought I had to be, then I would not be accepted.

That was the bondage of self. And now I was beginning to understand that if I could be released from that bondage, if I could lay down the fear, I could blossom into my full self. I could become what Spirit had been whispering to me all along. This was the will of God of my understanding.

From my journal during this period:

I want to manifest a new life for myself… I want to be comfortable in my skin and in my life. I need to not feel responsible for Rich's happiness. I need to continue to let go of control. I'm only in control of me, and I surrender that control to Spirit. Guide me with an open heart.

The Call to Ministry

For my 50th birthday in January of 2020, just before the COVID shutdown, I celebrated with an amazing, joy-filled sober birthday party. Family and friends surrounded me from every area of my life, including the community at the church where I was now working. It was a special evening, filled with love, laughter, and a sense of being deeply cared for.

One of the gifts I received was seed money to begin the path toward ministerial school. It had been in the back of my mind for a long time, and now, after coming through my dark night of the soul, I was ready to hear what had been calling me. I used that seed money to sign up for my first class to become a Unity minister. It felt like the natural next step, even though I knew it would take years of study and require a significant investment.

Almost immediately after enrolling, I had a conversation with a woman at my church who shared her experience of becoming a metaphysical minister. She told me how much she had enjoyed the process. Unlike the Unity program, it was a self-study path that took much less time and was far more affordable. I knew instantly that this was the right choice for me.

The timing was perfect. I dropped the Unity class, received a refund, and enrolled in the Metaphysical University program, feeling a profound certainty that I was exactly where I was meant to be.

All of this unfolded just before the pandemic began. When the world shut down and everything became quiet, I was able to step right into a new and transformative routine that was in alignment with my new path, and I loved every moment of it. Each morning, I woke up early with excited anticipation, eager to dive into my spiritual studies before beginning my online work from home. The teachings were speaking to a knowing within me that was coming alive in ways I could not have ever dreamed.

The Gift of the Pandemic

I was six months into working at the spiritual center when Covid-19 hit and everything shifted. That season marked the beginning of the next phase of my journey.

The shutdown was actually a gift for me. I know that for many, Covid was complicated and painful, but I often say it was like a magnifying glass. Whatever was already happening in your life, it magnified it.

By then, Rich and I were beginning to see healthier changes in our relationship, almost two years into sobriety. We were adjusting to life as empty nesters. Bodhi had moved back into town after finishing his two years of community college, and just days before the shutdown, he had driven off to California with his best friend and their dogs to take a job as the marketing director for a small company in Sacramento.

Alex was living with his girlfriend and working for Rich. Things were not perfect, but they were stable enough. He had a place to be, and that gave me a sense of relief.

And although Rich and I still had very different ideas about how our sons should do many parts of their lives, we had made an agreement in our recovery to stop having them be our main and almost only topic of communication.

We were coming to terms with the fact that we had to let them go and find their own way and our fighting over what we thought was only harming our relationships. That sometimes meant that we did not have anything to say to each other and allowing that sometimes awkward silence was part of our healing.

So when everything came to a sudden stop in March of 2020, I was grateful. Grateful for the pause. Grateful that I had a job where we could shift everything online. And grateful that all the skills I had gathered from years of work allowed me to truly be of service, helping the church continue to support and serve the community in a time when people needed it most.

Our church had already offered livestreamed services, so when the shutdown happened, we were ready. I was able to be part of the Sunday service as a member of the music team, and I also helped make all the classes available on Zoom.

I felt a deep sense of pride and a sense of oneness with the community and staff, knowing I could help support them through a time that was frightening and uncertain.

But at the same time, everything became still and quiet.

There were no constant distractions, no endless things to do. It was not about rushing to AA or Al-Anon meetings. It was not about another music rehearsal. It was not about going, going, going. Everything stopped. And in that stopping, I was being given the gift of space and the space to breathe, the space to listen, and the space to take the next steps in my Recover Your Soul journey.

Finding the Inner Sanctuary

I found a peace within myself that I had never touched before, a peace that had always been there but was hidden beneath the noise of distraction. For so long, I had been consumed with everything and everyone else, too busy to step into the inner sanctuary of my own heart where I could be still and connect with my Higher Self.

Something extraordinary began to happen as I immersed myself in those ministerial studies. I felt an opening, a releasing, a trusting, a remembering. It was a part of me that had always existed, but I had been afraid to let it thrive. Afraid to let go. Afraid to surrender.

It was during these studies that the third line of the Step Three Prayer began to take shape in me: "Take away my difficulties, that victory over them may bear witness to those I would help with Your Power, Your Love, and Your Way of Life. May I do Your will always."

All my life, I had resisted what I perceived as difficulty. I had lived in fear of struggle, doing everything I could to avoid it. What I had missed was the truth that difficulty is not a punishment. It is part of being human. Life itself is complicated, and every challenge carries something to teach us.

As I healed from addiction and codependency, I began to recognize that each experience I had gone through, no matter how painful, had also given me insight and strength. By letting go of resistance, I began to feel more connected to the God of my understanding.

I came to see that as we show up in the fullness of who we are and as we show up healed, whole, and connected to something Greater Still, what once felt like difficulty can be reframed as a challenge. And from that place, our lives themselves become a witness. Not to fix others. Not to change them. But to stand in our authentic selves so that others can see what is possible.

That is the power of this line of prayer. When we allow Spirit to "take away" not the challenge itself but the belief that the challenge is difficult, we invite those around us to witness another way of being. They see us strong and grounded, not collapsing under pressure or falling back into old patterns. In turn, they are reminded that they can trust a higher power and that they too can live in alignment with a way of life that supports their fullest expression. **The greatest way to help another is not to save them but to bear witness to their wholeness by living from our own. The greatest way we can help another is to heal ourselves.**

Recover Your Soul

I was still reflecting on the vision I had created in my Prosperity Class in early 2019, knowing that if I truly wanted to reach those goals, I needed to begin taking action steps toward them as the class had taught. An idea had been stirring in me, something that wanted to take shape as a podcast or a blog. I had no idea what I was doing or where it would lead, but I knew I no longer wanted fear to drive my decisions.

I wanted to step out in faith, to take risks, and to trust that the next steps would be revealed as I walked forward.

The first question was what to call it. In October of 2019, while on a camping trip with Rich and Bodhi, I was in the car talking with Bodhi about this idea that had been pulling at me. Having studied marketing, he began asking me sharp, thoughtful questions to help me clarify my vision.

As we talked, the words *Recover Your Soul* came out of my mouth. The moment I spoke them, I felt chills run through me. I knew Spirit had given me that name, and with it, a sense of purpose.

At the time, I did not understand the depth of those words. Over time, they have continued to unfold as a gift from something Greater Still. The awareness is simple yet profound: **When we let go, when we stop being afraid and stop living from our old beliefs, patterns, and stories, and when we allow Spirit to take the lead, and we remain curious, open, and willing to awaken, we are being invited to recover our soul.**

By May of 2020, I began to speak and share my soul recovery journey with others. It was not because I set out to create a community, and it was certainly not because I wanted my name attached to it. I did not know what I was doing on any level. I was simply allowing myself to be Spirit-led, taking small actions that felt like whispers of inspiration.

Some of those whispers came through the voices of others, such as people at AA and Al-Anon meetings who told me, "There's just something about the way you share your stories. It is really impactful. You should share your story with more people."

Others came from the church and spiritual center where I worked, where people reflected back to me that my light and authenticity made a difference in their lives. I had always wanted to share light with those I cared about and beyond, and now I was beginning to understand the difference between thinking it was my responsibility and understanding it is about letting go.

The God of My Understanding

Over the years, my journey has deepened as I have stepped into the role of an ordained spiritual metaphysical minister. I have studied many traditions, inspired by Unity New Thought, *A Course in Miracles*, Buddhism, other Eastern philosophies, Christianity, metaphysics, and too many other spiritual teachers and authors to name.

What I have come to understand is that there is so much more than we can possibly grasp, and now even science is beginning to confirm it. Science is showing us the quantum field, the technologies that expand our understanding, and the remarkable ways our brains actually work. At the heart of it all, it is about energy.

What once felt woo-woo, strange, or far out no longer feels so distant. The more I read, watch, and listen to teachings across traditions, the more I see the same essential message shining through: be the light and live from love, expressed in different tones, different languages, and different flavors.

I take what I need and leave the rest. I have given myself permission to establish the Higher Power of my own understanding, a gift that came to me through the 12-Step rooms. From that foundation, I have been able to create and cultivate a personal relationship with the God of my understanding. Now I can use the word God freely. Now I can speak it without fear or judgment, without the weight my grandmother's teachings once placed on me. I now choose to use the words Source, Spirit and Universe, but also find the word God to bring me comfort.

And interestingly, I now hold a great deal of compassion for her. She was only trying to help me. She wanted to save me, offering me what she believed with the sincerity of her heart and the love she carried for me. Once I stopped holding on to the hurt, I could see the beauty and light in her. She gave me the very best she had, even though it came wrapped in her own fears and beliefs.

Life Happening With You

I have heard it said over and over again from many different teachers and theologians: "Life is not happening to you. It is happening for you." Through the lens of metaphysics, through the lens of co-creation, and through the AA 3rd Step Prayer, I would offer an even deeper truth: "Life is happening with you."

I have come to see the Universal Spiritual Laws as one of the greatest gifts of my life. The awareness that what we think, feel, and believe shapes the very life we live. I began to recognize that how I feel on the inside is reflected in the life I experience on the outside.

These awakenings came sometimes slowly, sometimes suddenly, and they profoundly shifted my life. It has never been a straight line. But from the very beginning, those changes were what I longed to share through the *Recover Your Soul* podcast. Not to tell anyone how to live, not to claim the right way, but simply to remember wholeness. To remember my wholeness.

Through Recover Your Soul, through my stories, and through the process of walking a spiritual path toward a happy and healthy life, I have been given gift after gift. Tools. New ways of being. Unexpected opportunities. Each one expanding my awareness that I have always been held in the arms of Spirit.

I have never been alone. That little girl who thought she was not enough, that was never true. I can choose to see the world in a different light. I can choose to see through a new perception. I can choose how I show up. Spirit and my Higher Self have always been in the seat of guidance, and my only task is to take my place as copilot. Together, we will find the way. **Faith is not something you earn. It is already within you, waiting to be remembered.**

Working the Steps in Your Own Life

Recover Your Soul - STEP 4

4. Open to Co-Creating with a Higher Power

Explore What Higher Power Is for You: **Define and explore your personal relationship with Source, Spirit, God, Higher Consciousness, or Light.** *Connect with Your Higher Power:* **Begin to co-create your life with the Higher Power of your understanding, choosing compassion, authenticity, and trust.**

***

Step 4 in the Recover Your Soul Process is about opening your heart to the possibility that you are not alone, that there is something greater moving with you and through you. This is the turning point where we begin to shift from trying to manage everything ourselves into entering a sacred partnership.

For some, that greater presence may be called God. For others, it may be Spirit, Source, a Higher Consciousness, or simply Light. What matters is not the name, but the relationship. The Recover Your Soul journey reminds us that no one else can define this for you. It is yours to uncover, yours to nurture, and yours to trust.

When we allow ourselves to define our own connection with a Higher Power, we step into freedom. We realize we no longer need to control everything on our own. We can release the illusion of separation and remember that there is wisdom, love, and strength available to us in every moment.

And from that relationship flows the invitation to co-create your life. To live in alignment with your soul's truth. To choose authenticity instead of fear, surrender instead of struggle, and trust instead of control.

This is the essence of Step 4: opening to partnership with something greater and discovering that life is not happening to you or for you, but with you.

As you Recover Your Soul, this step is not about giving yourself away. It is about reclaiming your power by remembering you are already whole, already connected, and already guided. **Spirit is always walking beside you, and your healing becomes an act of co-creation.**

If you'd like to go deeper into Step 4 and hear more of my personal journey with opening to co-creation, I've shared about this powerful process in several episodes of the *Recover Your Soul* Podcast. These conversations and reflections bring the step to life, not as an abstract idea, but as a lived experience.

Podcasts About Being Open to Co-Creating with a Higher Power

https://recoveryoursoulbook.com/

CHAPTER 6

Releasing the Old Beliefs

Old stories aren't truth. They're echoes, and we can choose when to stop listening. - RH

You may be thinking, OK, it sounds nice to feel connected to the Universe and in the flow, but how do you actually let go of old beliefs in the subconscious? That's a great question. And like all healing and awakening, it's a layered process. Each step down the path asks you to go a little deeper. For me, that path unfolded as I worked the 12 Steps of AA and Al-Anon and deepened my own spiritual practice recovering my soul.

Even as I was experiencing a spiritual awakening within my heart, releasing my old stories of pain didn't come naturally. I could feel the tug and had a quiet knowing that the more I let go, the more fully I could step into myself. Yet fear and resistance clung tightly, as those old patterns feel hard to break. I wasn't sure how to actually "do" the work of healing.

My journals from that time are filled with pages of doubt: not being sure of myself, feeling inadequate, being afraid of disappointing, and being afraid of not being enough. I worried about my family, about whether it was really OK to detach. And yet alongside all of that fear was a persistent call from my Higher Self to discover more of who I really was outside of my wounds and old beliefs.

One journal entry captures it well:

> *My life is completely constricted with fear. Not able to feel and*
> *be in the moment, not able to be adventurous, not trusting*
> *that I will be safe... I get caught up in my head. I want to move*
> *past the fear, and trust my Higher Self.*

It was in returning again and again to my list of character defects and recognizing the protection they had once provided that I began to see the truth: Healing is not about judging or fixing myself, but about willingness. Willingness to release what no longer serves.

We hear that phrase often in spirituality: Let go of what no longer serves you. But what does that really mean? What does serve us? How do we tell the difference? I hadn't known for years because I was living from a reactionary, wounded place. Slowly, though, I began to see that what serves us is anything that moves us closer to love, wholeness, and trust. What no longer serves is whatever keeps us bound to fear, scarcity, and smallness.

The Fear of Change

It was becoming clear that I was still afraid to step into my whole, healed self. I feared that if I made big changes and if I dared to trust the voice calling me into more, I might lose everything I had known before. And even though much of what I had known was painful and needed to be released, it was still familiar. Familiarity can feel safer than freedom. **I was being invited to move past fear into discomfort, to risk trusting that if I let go of my old beliefs and protections, I would not only be OK, but I would be closer to the fullness of who I was created to be.**

That was the heart of Step Six in AA. It wasn't enough to recite the words and ask God to remove my character defects; I had to hand them over. I had to trust that what I released would be replaced with something greater, that being self-love and inner peace.

On the day I worked this step and read the Sixth Step prayer in the Big Book, I adjusted it just a bit in my own words, and like the vision practice I'd learned in Prosperity Plus, it was something I had to return to daily, allowing it to seep deeper into me.

Here is what guided me as I began to find my own voice and connection to my Higher Self:

> *God, I am now willing that You remove from me every single defect of character that stands in the way of my connection and usefulness to You and the world. Give me strength as I go out from here and to follow Your guidance, so I may be a light and a messenger of love in the world.*

This step of being entirely ready to let God remove my defects sounds so straightforward. But the truth is, letting go is hard. My old patterns were well-worn tools: being withdrawn, self-seeking, defensive, fearful, judgmental, anxious, isolated, masked, and selfish. Even victimhood and control had once felt like safety. They were habits that had shielded me from pain.

And yet, life kept offering me opportunity after opportunity to surrender them. To stop clinging and to get off the emotional battlefield. To trust that what once protected me was no longer needed. Each release was an act of faith, and each act of faith carried me closer to freedom.

The Power of Forgiveness and Amends

It was really through the power of forgiveness that the next part of my healing opened. Forgiveness, self-compassion, and the practice of amends, all so central to the 12 Steps, were the doorways that allowed me to begin releasing the old armor I had carried. These practices reminded me that it is possible to forgive ourselves, to ask forgiveness from others for the ways we have shown up, and to make new choices in how we live and the tools we reach for.

Every day I asked for grace. That is what Step Seven in AA offers: "Humbly ask Him to remove our shortcomings." It was about choosing progress over perfection, choosing to walk one more step toward a more awakened life with humility and grace.

Which naturally led me into AA's Steps Eight and Nine, respectively:

- "Made a list of all persons we had harmed, and became willing to make amends to them all."

- "Made direct amends to such people whenever possible, except when to do so would injure them or others."

I wasn't someone who had left a trail of wreckage behind me in the way some in the rooms had. But if I were honest, I had participated in the pain within my own family. I had unconsciously reacted from my character defects there. Even when my intentions were "good," even when I thought I was being helpful or kind, I had actually been trying to control them or the outcome. I had built systems of passive aggression. And in my marriage, I had been part of creating a relationship where neither of us felt truly safe, loved, or seen.

In our darkest years, Rich couldn't feel loved or accepted by me, and I couldn't feel loved or accepted by him. We had created not a home, but a battleground. And it was time to lay our weapons down. **Forgiveness isn't about forgetting the pain. It's about remembering who you are without it.**

Making Amends in Mexico

In our pre-pandemic trip to Mexico, on that beautiful miracle of a Law of Attraction adventure where we found ourselves eating tacos by the sea, it became unmistakably clear: it was time for me to make my AA amends to Rich. I had harmed him by the way I had shown up in our relationship. And now it was time to take full responsibility and allow him to see that.

It was time to say the words I had resisted for so long: I am sorry.

In the past, I had rarely spoken those words. I had been too entangled in resentment and control, too invested in being "right," to admit the harm I had caused. But one evening, standing together and looking out over the ocean, I finally felt the humility rise in me.

With sincerity and trembling honesty, I told him I knew how I had hurt him and that I had wielded the threat of leaving as a weapon in our arguments, a tool of control I knew would wound him. And then I told him, from the deepest place in my heart, "I am sorry."

Rich received my words with gratitude. He acknowledged how painful that pattern had been for him, how it had left scars on his experience of our marriage. In that moment, I felt released and a new freedom. It was small but powerful. It was the beginning of a new kind of safety between us, a space where healing could take root.

My perception was shifting, and I was willing to take accountability for my side of the story. For so long, I had been obsessed with pointing out what was wrong with everyone else, blind to my own part.

Making amends wasn't about blame or shame or even guilt. It was about something deeper: the courage to recognize how pain shapes our behaviors, the willingness to stop hiding behind those defenses, and the desire to choose a new way of seeing it and a new way of showing up.

This moment invited me to see clearly the systems my younger self had built to protect me from the world, systems of control, withdrawal, and passive aggression, and to finally ask the harder questions:

- What is my part?
- How am I contributing to the problem?
- What am I willing to let go of so I can move forward?

In truth, we were both addicts. Each carrying our own addictions, wounds, stories, and coping strategies. But in that moment in Mexico, with AA and Al-Anon holding us both, I began to see that our healing could happen together and there could be healing from a painful past.

Living Amends

As I walked further into this journey, I began to realize the incredible power of gentleness, especially toward the younger, wounded parts of myself. This part of the 12-Step path was not about going around and telling everyone how sorry I was. It was deeper than that. It was about showing up differently. It was about living in alignment with my authentic Higher Self. It was about living amends.

A living amends goes beyond words. It's not just about apologies. It's about embodying change. It's about allowing authenticity to infuse every corner of your life and choosing to let your actions speak where words alone could never be enough.

These amends don't belong only to the season when you're formally working through a program. They become a way of life, a daily offering of responsibility. This is where Step 10 in AA comes alive: "Continued to take personal inventory, and when we were wrong, promptly admitted it." It's the practice of real-time honesty with ourselves and others.

But let's be honest. Vulnerability and accountability are not easy. Life will still press on those old "value buttons": insecurity, doubt, fear of not being enough. It can feel like the world is triggering us. Yet I came to understand that the power doesn't lie in avoiding triggers or blaming the outside world. The power lies in recognizing those buttons for what they are as leftovers from old belief systems. and choosing to release them. To let go of what no longer serves. **Old stories aren't truth. They're echoes, and we can choose when to stop listening.**

That choice, made again and again, is what makes a living amends. It's what transforms an apology into a new way of being.

A Course in Miracles

In February of 2021, my church offered a year-long class on *A Course in Miracles*. I had heard about this book for nearly 30 years but had never opened its pages. Now, as I was nearing the end of my ministerial studies and fresh from completing the 12 Steps with my sponsor, the timing felt perfect.

Step 11 in AA had already planted the instruction in me:

"Sought through prayer and meditation to improve our conscious contact with God as we understood Him, praying only for knowledge of His will for us and the power to carry that out."

I knew I was being called deeper.

A Course in Miracles, first published in 1975, is a channeled text of spiritual teachings often studied in groups because of its complexity. Even after years of metaphysical study, I found it challenging to unravel on my own and wanted to connect to others as I dug into this new layer of study. So for a year I worked with a study group through my church, and I was grateful to have the support of a group to help me work through the lessons. At this time I also signed up for a year of daily videos from Marianne Williamson, who later joined me on my podcast and is one of the best-known teachers of *A Course in Miracles.*

The central message of the *Course* is simple, though not easy: to move from fear to love and to release the judgment and pain that come from feeling separate from God.

For me, raised in a Buddhist tradition, the Christian language and imagery felt foreign. It took months of sitting with the text before I could hear the truth underneath the words.

And yet, that was the very point. *A Course in Miracles* mirrored so much of my life. I was used to seeing and hearing through the filter of old perceptions and beliefs. But when I was willing to open, to look again, and to see with fresh eyes, something powerful shifted. The way I perceived reality itself began to change.

What moved me most was the *Course*'s teaching on judgment. I began to ask new questions:

- What if I stopped labeling everything as right or wrong?
- What if I stopped judging my family as right or wrong?
- What if I stopped judging myself as right or wrong? What if I let go of blame and grievance completely?

And perhaps most radical of all:

- What if fear itself were not an ultimate truth but just a lens I had been choosing to look through?
- What if I could choose to see everything differently?

That single shift, choosing to see differently, became a key that unlocked everything.

Choosing Love over Fear

What I noticed is that this practice began to open up space within me, a space where I could finally see my own experience with a depth of compassion and tenderness I had never experienced before. For so long,

I had been caught up in the need to protect myself, to prove myself, all of it tied to that core belief that everyone else needed to come before me and that I could not rely on anyone else to love me the way that I wanted or needed. That it was not safe to open myself completely to the people around me, even the ones I loved the most.

They were the stories of a little girl. A little girl who got in trouble. A little girl who was rejected. A little girl who was told she was not smart, who heard messages that she was not enough somehow

But now I could see those stories for what they were: not truth, only memories and interpretations. I wanted so desperately to move out of that old place and into something new. I wanted to stop living from those younger aspects of self. I no longer wanted to bring to the world the tools of withdrawal, self-righteousness, control, enabling, or fear.

Those tools were no longer helpful. And it was through being brave enough to show up in my fully authentic and loving self that I felt I could set them down.

That practice was metaphysical. It was spiritual. It was a declaration: I am not here to be smaller. I am here to be fuller. I am here to expand, to know that I am whole exactly as I am. Whatever stories I tell myself about not being enough, they are only stories. And what I look for in this world, I will find.

Brené Brown captures this beautifully in her book, *Braving the Wilderness*: "Stop searching for proof that you don't belong – you'll always find it. True belonging lives in your heart, not in the world's evaluation. No one belongs here more than you."

If you want proof that you are not enough, the world will hand it to you. But if you want proof that you are wonderful, the world will hand you that, too. As I studied, journaled, and unpacked my own psyche, I began to see how true this was.

When I looked at my marriage only through the lens of what was wrong, I received more of what was wrong. But when I looked at my husband as a man who was deeply dedicated to his family and who also carried his own stories and struggles, I could meet him in a place of compassion. From there, we could both grow, and in our case, we were both dedicated to finding growth and healing.

It did not mean that there were still not behaviors or interactions that were hard at times, but I was able to see them from a healthier lens and not let them take me down a dark road of disappointment. **When I looked at my children, I began to see the wholeness of their souls, the beauty already in them.**

I chose to make amends to them too, not only in words, but through a living amends by becoming the kind of person I wanted them to experience as their mother. And as I shifted, they responded in kind. I admitted the harm that I had caused them not only in my drinking but also in my over-fixing and constant attempt to control their lives and choices.

They were both gracious and kind and said that my drinking had not been a harmful memory in their lives, aside from a few times of seeing me sick in the bathroom as children and not understanding what was wrong with me. They also said they had always felt that my intention behind my codependent behaviors had come from love.

I appreciated their kindness, knowing that they would need to unpack some of their feelings and desire to protect me later in their journey of healing.

Of course, that does not mean the world stopped pressing on me. Life will always keep pushing and showing up in its complexity and challenge. **Our triggers are powerful. But they are also invitations and opportunities to see the places where there is still work to be done.** And I still had work to do.

Seeing our Assets

When we do the work of acknowledging our character defects in Step Six of AA, the worksheet we are given pairs each defect with an asset. For every shortcoming, there is an antidote, a new tool we can reach for as we move forward. This practice reflects the spiritual principle of asking and receiving. We ask to have the bondage of self lifted, and in return, we are given what we need. Ask and you shall receive.

At the same time, *A Course in Miracles* was teaching me that at every moment, we are making a choice: love or fear. I began to see how the 12-Step practice of naming our defects and assets was another way of making that choice.

I could show up in the world from the place of my defect, driven by upset, control, and fear. Or I could choose the asset or the higher ground and show up as my authentic self. Both were tools, but one came from fear and the other from love.

The more I studied, the more I saw how often I had confused the two. I believed I was being loving when I acted from codependency or control, when I tried to manage the people around me or fix their problems. But underneath, I was afraid. Afraid of losing, afraid of being abandoned, afraid it would all fall apart, afraid of not being enough. **That fear drove me into behaviors that created deep suffering for myself and for those I loved.**

Being human means having feelings. Our emotions are essential and important. They are part of the gift of being alive. But suffering comes when we resist what is, when we demand that things be different than they are. And that suffering is not inevitable. It is a choice.

Another Layer of Awareness

I was so proud and excited to have become an ordained metaphysical minister. I had begun to share my journey in the podcast, and it was slowly growing, and I had even given my first guest sermon at church. I still did not know exactly what was next for me, but I felt deeply called into leadership and into helping others discover how to recover their soul.

Life had settled into a new kind of normal. We were meeting again in person post-Covid shutdown, and they were smaller services, but face-to-face. I felt confident in my role at the church. Yet underneath, a familiar gritty pattern was stirring in my relationship with my supervisor. I could hear an echoing of issues I had faced years before as an office manager. That confused me, because I had been doing so much inner work and believed I was showing up in healthier ways.

What I did not see at the time was that I was about to be given another opportunity to meet those sneaky subconscious beliefs and defensive character defects. A few conversations about my job description, such as whether I was meeting their expectations, triggered something deep within me.

Suddenly, I was back in old territory. First, comfortable and appreciated, then questioned, then feeling like the ground was being pulled out from under me. The pain of it was sharp. And I found myself slipping back into my old habits, revealing my defects and defensive patterns.

I did not like being criticized. I could see myself becoming that little girl again, the one afraid of getting in trouble, desperate to prove herself, and convinced she was about to be rejected and harmed. I spiraled between sadness, confusion, anger, and blame, bouncing between my Higher Self, who longed to release old wounds, and the wounded parts of me that felt judged and wronged. My "value button" was being pushed hard.

During that crisis, I wrote in my journal:

I'm confused. I'm avoiding the ability to feel my heart and soul, back to a shrew. Back to a place of abandonment and fear when all I want is to be loved.

That word "shrew" from the prayer chaplain came back to me and pierced through my defenses like lightning. It stung, because when what we believe about ourselves feels attacked, it always hurts. But as the word echoed in me, I could see on an even deeper level my controlling nature, my fixing, my dissatisfaction for what they truly were not righteous stands, not justified responses, but tender patterns I had carried for protection. **Patterns that had quietly been eroding my relationships, even as I believed they were keeping me safe.**

The Abraham Hicks Miracle

This was when I had another mini miracle, a reminder that when we ask, we will receive. I was at the gym working out and decided to listen to a podcast. Without my glasses, I couldn't see the screen clearly, but one of the suggested choices on Spotify was Abraham Hicks. I had heard the name before and assumed it was an older man. I clicked play, and out came the voice of a middle-aged woman, Esther Hicks, translating the teachings of the energy she calls Abraham. The title of the episode was "How to Handle Criticism."

Wow. A message spoken directly to me at the exact moment I needed it.

That 15-minute talk was a gift. Abraham explained that feeling criticized is not just about the judgment we sense from others. It is also about the judgment we carry toward them and the way we compound our own suffering by fighting against it, trying to control a person or a situation that is not ours to control. In my need for things to be different, I was giving my power away.

This teaching, along with what I was learning in *A Course in Miracles*, cracked something open in me. I began to see how much I was still clinging to my desire to please, my need for approval, and my unconscious attachment to old beliefs. I could see how often I was still reaching for the unhealthy tools and how my unhealthy habits that had once felt like protection were now only hurting me.

Resentment. Defensiveness. The constant need to explain myself. These habits were not benefiting me. Even after all the healing work I had done, I was still holding tightly to fear. At my job, I watched myself in real time become defensive, convinced I was under attack, and certain I was right. I saw my old self take the wheel. And she is intense. She wants it her way. She wants to be accepted and valued She wants to be loved.

But in this moment, I learned something life-changing: the value of not having to prove I was right. What if the real importance was not about convincing anyone else, but about knowing what was true for me?

I began to realize even more deeply that if I let go of my patterns, beliefs, and old tools, I might not get what I thought I wanted. And what if that was OK? What if surrender opened me to something better than what I was grasping for? What if connecting to my Higher Power meant I could trust that everything was already working out for me and to let go of the outcome.

The Sneakiness of Control

Control is a sneaky, sneaky thing. It rises up and reclaims ground before we even realize it. I thought I was on a new path, a new journey. So much in my life was changing for the better, and yet in upset, hurt, and conflict, it still found its way in.

That was when I remembered the third line of the prayer from Step Three in AA:

"Take away my difficulties, that victory over them may bear witness to those I would help of Your power, Your love, and Your Way of Life."

This was another layer being revealed around my resistance to what was uncomfortable and painful. What if I released the fear of getting in trouble? What if I allowed someone to think poorly of me or to disagree with what I was doing? What if I didn't take their opinion of me personally? What if I didn't fall into old patterns of people-pleasing or attempt to control?

What if I was not actually doing the right thing? What if the job I was doing was not the job they wanted from me?

It was fascinating to watch myself wrestle with these questions, to feel the criticism sting, and then to realize that even this was an invitation. It was a chance to let go. To release self-righteousness and defense. To soften and surrender to my healing process on an even deeper level.

It is interesting how, when life begins moving toward what we want, we often respond by holding even tighter to what we know. We convince ourselves we are not controlling, but the very act of clinging is proof that we are and that we are being ruled by old fear. Attempting to control the path is choosing fear over love.

I was gaining traction as a speaker at local spiritual centers and had begun to offer spiritual coaching through *Recover Your Soul*, and that community was coming alive through the podcast. Yet there was still fear around stepping out in faith and trusting that I could support my financial commitment to my family on this new path. But this was an invitation to feel, learn, and grow beyond what felt comfortable.

And so, when I finally gave notice at the job that had both challenged me and held me at a church I had attended for more than 20 years, I knew it was the right choice. I could trust what was next, even if I did not yet know what it would be.

I leaned on my spiritual tools to process the experience, learn from it, and practice forgiveness for myself and for them.

An opening to Forgiveness

Forgiveness did not come easily to me. At that point in my journey, I was still fresh in recovering my soul and still carrying resentment and blame. I believed I had been wronged in countless ways by my family, by my marriage, and by life itself, and those wounds felt justified. But I was also beginning to see that holding on to those grievances was only hurting me. They were keeping me bound to the very pain I longed to be free from, preventing me from living the life I wanted.

When I began studying *A Course in Miracles*, something shifted in me. Its constant reminder that the path is to move from fear to love and that forgiveness is the key, felt radical. I wasn't ready to live it fully, but I could feel a door cracking open.

What if forgiveness wasn't about excusing anyone else's behavior but about setting myself free? What if I could stop replaying every slight? What if I could stop needing life and the people in it to unfold exactly the way I thought they should? What if forgiveness was less about them and more about healing the wounds inside of me?

I didn't know how to do it. But I knew something had to shift, and I could feel my Higher Power coming online and leading the way. So I pulled out my list of character defects again. I named them honestly: withdrawn, fearful, controlling, and self-seeking.

I could see how I had been clinging to those defenses because I didn't trust that I could survive without them. They felt familiar. They felt safe. **And yet I was beginning to believe that if I let them go, Spirit might give me something greater in return.**

It was just a glimpse, just the beginning of opening to forgiveness. But even that glimpse was a door, a door into the possibility that I could lay down my weapons, release my resentments, and let the little girl inside of me finally rest.

Rich's Sobriety Journey

Rich's sobriety has been its own journey, and for a long time, I thought we were doing this together. When he had three years of sobriety under his belt, I thought, "We've got it now. We're safe." But then he started drinking occasionally, quietly. He didn't tell me, but I had a knowing that there was something going on. When he finally came and told me the truth, the old me would have spiraled into anger, fear, and ultimatums. But by then, I had been working my 12 Step program, along with the 9-Step Recover Your Soul Process that was developing .

I saw it differently. I saw the addict in him navigating his own path, stumbling toward his own healing. And I realized: It was not my job to manage it, to control it. His journey was his. My journey was mine. He would repeat this pattern for a few years, and eventually, he chose sobriety again for himself. That was his decision, not mine. And for me, the healing was in knowing that my peace did not depend on what was in his glass.

During these years, and the many slips that Rich had in those years, my gratitude was that there was a new, healthier communication between us because we had been working so hard on creating safety in our relationship. I had once used the term "trust" to mean that he would do what I wanted or needed to feel safe, but now I could see that was actually a form of control.

Safety was the most important element in my relationship, and that gave him the space to slip and fall and make the decision to come back to sobriety without my demands or how I thought he should do it. He did not ever go back to AA, but he was on his own path to recover his soul, and although it looked very different from the path I was walking, it was a path in the same direction.

I was powerless over his addiction, but I was not powerless over how I could choose to see him and his journey, and I was determined to release the old patterns and stories about his addiction and who I wanted him to be. My trust was no longer in trying to control him, but in trusting that my Higher Power and my Higher Self were guiding my path.

Who Would I Be without My Old Story?

Who would I be without my old story? That question haunted me – and called to me. For so long, my identity had been bound to the old beliefs, stories, and patterns of codependency and pleasing people. But something deeper was rising within me, urging me to loosen my grip and let go.

The life I lived before hasn't been erased. It happened. It shaped me. But I no longer have to let it define me. Slowly, layer by layer, I've been learning to release the judgment of others, yes, but mostly of myself. That release has been one of the most profound offerings of forgiveness in my life. A forgiveness of everything and everyone, a forgiveness that keeps unfolding, like waves smoothing the rough edges of a stone.

To see that forgiveness is beyond the pain, hurt, and blame. It was letting go of the stories I held onto so tightly that I had created from those experiences and feelings and seeing that there is purpose in the painful experiences. Seeing that I can choose how I will see and remember it, and that when my perception shifts, so does the energy around those memories. Forgiveness was seeing beyond the story and recovering the experiences of the soul from wholeness instead of pain.

It hasn't been sudden. It has come in quiet increments, like a tide rising inside me. And perhaps the greatest gift of this process has been in my marriage. For years, I carried resentment that my husband had never made a traditional AA amends to me as part of his healing journey. That silence hurt.

But as I began to forgive myself, to offer grace to the wounded parts within me, something unexpected happened: the door to grace opened wider. And that grace spilled outward, softening me, allowing me to extend compassion, empathy, and acceptance not only to him but to everyone.

Forgiveness has never meant pretending the pain wasn't real. Acceptance has never meant approval. It doesn't erase what happened or mean that I have to like it. What it does mean is that I can choose to see it differently. I can hold it as part of a larger journey, something greater than I can fully understand, something that has also carried me here, to this moment of awakening.

That shift has been the real miracle, realizing that I can make a different decision. I get to choose how I see my life, my relationships, and my past. *A Course in Miracles* and other spiritual teachings affirmed what my soul already knew, that perception is not fixed. I no longer have to look through the eyes of my old patterns, fears, or wounds. We can choose again.

I am choosing to see through the eyes of love. **Forgiveness isn't about forgetting the pain. It's about remembering who you are without it.**

Working the Steps in Your Own Life

Recover Your Soul - STEP 5

5. Release Old Patterns That No Longer Serve You
Cultivate Awareness and Insight: **Use your growing awareness to gain insight into your old patterns and beliefs, and to recognize what you have learned from them.** *Practice Compassion and Forgiveness:* **Release these patterns through awareness, compassion, and forgiveness both toward yourself and others so you can make space for healing, peace, and new ways of being.**

***

Releasing old patterns is not a one-time choice but a living practice. It begins with awareness and seeing clearly the beliefs, stories, and patterns that shaped you. With awareness comes insight, and with insight comes the courage to ask: Does this still serve me?

Often, those patterns were born as protectors. They kept you safe, helped you survive, and gave you a way to navigate a world that felt uncertain. But what once kept you safe may now keep you small. What once helped you cope may now block your growth.

The invitation of Step 5 in the Recover Your Soul Process is not to judge or condemn these parts of yourself, but to meet them with compassion. Here, forgiveness becomes the key. First, forgiveness of self for the ways you have shown up in fear, control, or resentment and then forgiveness that extends outward to others. Forgiveness does not erase the past, nor excuse what happened. It transforms the way you carry it. It loosens the grip of shame, softens the chains of fear, and makes space for love to take root.

Each time you release what no longer serves, you create more space inside – space for clarity, authenticity, and connection. Old stories lose their hold. New ways of being begin to emerge. Step by step, you return to the truth of who you really are: whole, worthy, and free.

When you choose compassion over judgment, forgiveness over resentment, and love over fear, you are no longer bound by the patterns that once defined you. You begin to live not from the wounds of the past, but from the light of your Higher Self. This is the freedom offered by Recover Your Soul Step 5.

If you feel called to go deeper, I invite you to listen to these *Recover Your Soul* podcast episodes, where I share more of my story, along with tools and reflections, to support you on your own path of releasing and becoming.

Podcasts About Releasing Old Patterns

https://recoveryoursoulbook.com/

Writing a New Story

The story I tell myself becomes the life I live. So now I choose love, peace, and possibility. - RH

We live in a story. Of course we do. Every thought we think, every action we take, every book we read, or movie we watch is woven from a story. It is how the human brain makes sense of the world. From the time we were little, we were surrounded by stories. Our parents read tales to us that ended with "and they lived happily ever after." We heard stories that carried warnings, stories that sparked adventure, and stories with a beginning, a middle, and an end.

In the same way, we grow up telling ourselves stories about who we are, about what happened to us, about what life means. Over time, we often keep adding new chapters that quietly reinforce those old versions, even when they no longer reflect who we are becoming.

For me, a story I had been carrying was that I was not traditionally smart. Another story I had been carrying was that I was not enough. And I had been carrying the story that it was my job to fix everyone else, that I was responsible for their pain and their healing. These stories lived in my mind like a constant hum. They pulled from my past and consumed my present, all in an effort to control what might happen in the future.

But what if we stopped to listen more carefully? What if we paid attention not only to the story we are repeating to ourselves, but to the story we are actively creating? What if we chose to take responsibility for the story of our own lives that we tell of the past and create for the future?

Awakening to New Possibilities

Throughout my spiritual awakening, I began to understand the power of thought, feeling, and belief. What I thought, felt, and believed were creating the very experience I was living. And in any given moment, I could choose: I could stay in the old pain and the victim story, or I could step forward into creating and living a new story. A hero's story.

I returned to my character defects card again because it holds such an important reminder. In AA, we ask God to remove these defects, these shortcomings. But we do not stop there. We ask to be moved into the space of our true and whole self. We ask to be made ready to stand in the fullness of who we are, to embrace our greatest potential, to accept our gifts, and to live from authenticity in a new story.

Healing and living in this new story comes from leaning into the assets on the other side of each defect, and updating our beliefs to match the truth of our authentic self and of our soul operating system. When I looked at the list of assets, not just glanced at it, but truly and deeply looked at it, I asked myself, "What if I lived my life from this potential? What would I do? Who could I be?"

From this place of wholeness and connection to Source, from this place of love, I saw that I could indeed become all of the things I had written in my Prosperity Plus class vision statement. And the following questions rose inside me: Could I really believe these things could come to me? Could I ask for even more? Could I dare to believe I was worthy of it all?

The list of assets became like a map, showing me the antidotes to pain and fear. It revealed new roles for the protectors I had relied on for so long. And these assets, these new tools, would be what I used to co-create the latest story of my life.

The assets were: outgoing, selfless, grateful, accepting, realistic, humble, modest, able to face problems, tolerant, respectful, open to criticism, honest, courageous, confident, kind, closed-mouthed, and secure.

From the new perception that opened through my awakening, I could see that these qualities were not just words on a page. They were truths. They were who I had always been from my Higher Self and the ways I longed to be in the world, the ways I wanted to respond to whatever life placed in front of me. This list became a path to expansion, an invitation to meet everything in a new way.

Could I choose to show up with these qualities in every area of my life? Could I face each situation and respond from these aspects rather than from fear? As *A Course in Miracles* and **...spiritual studies kept reminding me the choice was always between love and fear.**

And I was ready to choose love. I was ready to live by these principles. I was ready to live as my authentic self.

This awareness enabled me to start writing a new story and update the beliefs that had previously held me back. My new story said, "I am smart. I am worthy. I am only responsible for my own feelings and happiness. I am enough. I am lovable. I am safe. I can always choose to live from love, and I can accept the love offered to me."

There was a deep shift happening within me. I was beginning to trust that these updated ways of seeing and believing were not only possible, but true. They could become my operating system. They could carry me into the life I wanted to create. They could empower me to face challenges from a position of strength instead of shrinking back into fear.

From my journal during my separation in December 2012, I saw the glimmers of this possibility:

> *I want to manifest a new life for myself. I want to grow and define deep confidence in myself, a foundation rooted in humility and gratitude. I want to accept the challenge to push against discomfort and see the truth. I want to love myself without fear of others' judgment or rejection. I want to connect deeply with this life and inspire those around me. I want to sing, to share my voice in song and in word.*

What had once seemed like desperate hope had become a concrete possibility.

The Tony Robbins Gift

About a month before I gave notice at my Unity Church in 2022 and stepped fully into being Rev. Rachel, devoting myself to the *Recover Your Soul* podcast, I was gifted a ticket to a four-day Tony Robbins virtual seminar called Unleash the Power Within. The timing could not have been more perfect. It arrived right as I was releasing old beliefs and stories that no longer served me and opening to a new perception of myself and the world.

Tony Robbins is masterful at what he does. In those four days, he guided us through a process that helped me fully recognize the stories I had been living in and the truth that if you change your story, you can change your life.

For me, the seminar was another reminder, another offering of support from the Universe and my Higher Self. The message was clear: It was time to change my story, and it was time to take the leap into creating a new life- even if I was unclear about what it was or how to get there.

Transformation in Family and Relationships

Speaking of stories, you may wonder what was happening with my family while I was undergoing this inner work and experiencing these profound shifts in perception. My family life continued with ups and downs, but my focus was shifting more and more toward my own healing. I was learning to use my new tools to detach with love so I could support my husband and sons as witnesses to their own journeys, without taking on responsibility for their choices or suffering their consequences.

Let's go back in time a bit to catch up with my family story. In May of 2020, my son Alex, still trying to navigate his life in Colorado, had a major blowup with his girlfriend, then another with his dad. It all came crashing down at once, and he decided he needed a significant change. Spirit often moves in those moments, doing for us what we cannot do for ourselves. But sometimes grace arrives in packages that look messy and painful at first. The very next day, Alex booked a one-way ticket and moved in with his brother who had been in California for a few months

That moment marked a new beginning for him, as well as for Rich and me. It was a fresh start for all of us, space to untangle from the dysfunction of our alcoholic family system. With physical distance came the possibility of releasing the old story and beginning to write a new one more easily for all of us.

Without the constant friction of daily interaction, we could each begin to step into new patterns. And here was the most essential truth: I was not responsible for their beliefs, patterns, and stories. I was only responsible for my own. It had been hard to let go when the kids were living close to us, but distance made it easier to detach and allow them to make their own choices and to face their own consequences.

They each had developed skills to make a living and needed to find their way into adulthood. This included their use of drugs and alcohol, as Bodhi had just turned 21 and Alex was 23. The apples had not fallen far from the tree, and although they had seen how destructive addiction had been in their family system, I would need to fully let go of their journey. That is the heart of what I have been learning in Al-Anon from the very beginning. The Seven Detachments remind us:

- Not to suffer because of the actions or reactions of other people.

- Not to allow ourselves to be used or abused in the name of someone else's recovery.

- Not to do for others what they can do for themselves.

- Not to manipulate situations so others will eat, sleep, work, pay bills, stop drinking, or behave as we think they should.

- Not to cover up another's mistakes or misdeeds.

- Not to create a crisis.

- Not to prevent a crisis that is inevitable in the natural course of events.

I had read this list almost every day for years, and through the work I had been doing, I was slowly releasing the obsessive thinking that had drained me for all those years and beginning to live from the wisdom detachment offered.

Through my new spiritual lens, I could finally see the vital importance of these principles. I was not responsible for what was happening in anyone else's life. What I could do was love compassionately and allow each person to make their own choices and live with the consequences. I did not have to live in the fear of those consequences but could allow myself to feel the feelings that washed over me as they experienced their own.

Forgiveness and compassion became my strengths, giving me the ability to love unconditionally while still detaching with love. My responsibility was to show up authentically in my relationships and circumstances. Theirs was to make their own choices and walk their own paths.

Stepping into my authentic and whole self required me to push back against the old doubts and fears that fueled my codependency and control. I was still nervous and uncertain about what the future would bring, but I could feel something deeper now. I was being guided and supported. And that felt both empowering and exciting.

Finding a Voice through My *Recover Your Soul* Podcast

This brings me back to the journey of the *Recover Your Soul* podcast and stepping out into the world as Rev. Rachel. I published my very first episode in May of 2020. At first, it was just me, speaking into a voice memo on my phone and uploading it to a hosting site. It was unedited, raw, and vulnerable. I had no idea what the long-range vision would be. All I knew was that I wanted to share my spiritual journey and transformation, weaving together the 12 Steps, spirituality, positive psychology, and life.

Of course, the old beliefs showed up. The familiar voice whispered that I was not smart enough to create a podcast. But my Higher Self whispered that was not the truth of who I was. I wanted to practice living into new beliefs, writing a new story.

Over the years, I had proven to myself that I loved learning systems and figuring out procedures and that I was good at it. I realized that creating a podcast was just an extension of that curiosity and love for learning. So I dove in. I researched everything I could find about podcasting. I stopped telling myself I couldn't and began telling myself that I could, and not only that, but I could do it well.

That shift led me to reexamine the old stories I had carried about myself. I began to find evidence of the opposite: proof of the truth about who I was and what I had accomplished. I reflected on the various things I had accomplished in my life and, for the first time, allowed myself to acknowledge what I was proud of. It felt strange and uncomfortable at first, but once I opened the door, I could see a lifetime of strength, courage, success, and worthiness staring back at me.

With each episode, I grew more confident. I learned how to record on my computer, how to edit, and how to shape the storyline of my message. But there was still a tension I had not yet resolved. I was walking a fine line around how much to share about my spiritual experience without directly mentioning AA or Al-Anon.

Out of respect for AA's 12 Traditions and their guidance around anonymity and promotion, I held back. Yet holding back kept me from fully telling my own story of recovery and what I was now calling Recover Your Soul.

Because for me, it was never only about sobriety through the 12 Steps. It was about something larger. It was about awakening. It was about reclaiming my soul. And I felt called to share openly, to say the words out loud, finally. I wanted to talk about all of it, not just AA or Al-Anon, not just the Unity Church where I had found community, but the way all of these threads were weaving together through my spiritual studies and personal awakening.

There was an intersection of ideas, practices, and truths that were transforming my life in profound ways, and it felt too important to keep quiet. What was taking shape in me was more than recovery. It was recovering my soul. A living puzzle of healing and awakening, coming together piece-by-piece into a picture of wholeness I had never known before.

I took that leap in the eighth episode, where I spoke about the Seven Detachments. At the time I was struggling with my constant worry over Alex, still slipping into behaviors the list warned against. I realized I could no longer avoid it. I needed to share the full truth of my journey. And that was the beginning of opening entirely into the voice of Recover Your Soul and all the parts of my healing journey.

That episode immediately jumped in downloads well beyond the few listens I was getting from family and friends. I recognized there was a calling, a real need for this work. I was not the only one living through these situations.

A spiritual transformation was happening within me that went beyond what the rooms of AA and Al-Anon can teach, because those spaces wisely stay within the scope of the 12 Steps and approved literature. That is the purpose of the traditions: to keep the programs from becoming diluted, but I needed to be outside of that scope

So I decided to share my full experience openly and without fear. I wanted to speak about spirituality on a broader scale alongside the powerful offerings from12 step work. I wanted to discuss *A Course in Miracles*, metaphysics, and the other ideas that were profoundly changing my life.

I wanted to speak directly about how a spiritual practice could help us truly let go of what no longer serves and how spiritual and metaphysical practices could bring peace into a messy life. As I did this, things began to align with the vision I had written in my Prosperity Plus class for a career, a vision that, at the time I could not see had a path forward.

Once I was sharing my story on the podcast, I became even more aware of the power of the stories we tell and the way we tell them. We all pass through painful and difficult times. That is the essence of the human condition. How we choose to be in those moments is a deliberate choice. How we choose to speak about them is a deliberate choice.

Even as I stepped more fully into sharing on the podcast, the old beliefs continued to surface. In March of 2021, I wrote about the familiar tension I felt after singing at church. Sometimes, after a full day at my church, I would come home feeling heavy from performing, and then the inner critic would arrive, asking if I was good enough and if I had sung well enough. That voice would try to tear me down, keep me small and safe.

I was still dancing between my Higher Self and my inner critic and learning to still the harsh voice of fear and choose grace and love.

I wrote in my journal:

Not sure where the music will take me, but I feel strongly that there is something there to hold onto even past my inner critic Wake up, be authentic. Be aware. Be kind. Be open. Open your heart. To feel alive and connected, to have a spiritual life, this is who I want to be

The calling was clear, even when the path was not yet visible.

Choosing Love over Past Pain

I had a very impactful experience one summer afternoon when Rich and I were driving home from the lake with a friend. It had been a beautiful Colorado day of wakeboarding, sunshine, and laughter. On the drive back, our friend casually asked how we had met. Rich and I perked up and began bantering, telling the story we love to share.

It was the story of him showing up as a friend's date for my 22nd birthday party, of all the little coincidences and perfect timing, of how, when we both found ourselves single, we noticed each other across a crowded room and then never left each other's side. The truck was filled with joy, connection, and the light of our love story.

But then, almost without thinking, I shifted into the pain story. I began talking about how he had abandoned me to work on the cabin, about our alcoholism, about years of difficulty with the kids, and the battles that scarred our marriage. I described the suffering of more than 20 years, ending with how I finally moved out with our oldest son. It was as if the air was sucked out of the truck. A heavy darkness filled the space, and I could see Rich's face clouded with hurt and confusion. When we dropped our friend off at her car, I was still in that energy, seeing my husband through the lens of those years of hardship.

Rich did not respond with anger. Instead, with gentle curiosity, he asked why I had chosen to tell her all of that, especially when it had not been asked for. His words pierced through my own confusion. I could feel the part of me that wanted to justify, but I also had new tools at my disposal. I took a breath, offered myself compassion, and asked Spirit to help me return to love.

Yes, those painful things happened. It is not about pretending they did not. But I realized that the difference lies in how I tell the story. I could tell it from pain and despair, or I could tell it from the perspective of empowerment and transformation, the hero's journey that shows what is possible when we choose healing. That insight is why, even in this book, I am mindful about the stories I share and the way I share them, and even choose to not tell them. My goal is not to relive the past as trauma but to show how we can look back with a new perception.

As I apologized to Rich that afternoon, I recognized something profound. At every moment, I have a choice in how I see him. When we shared our love story, I felt a deep sense of love and connection. When I told the pain story, I was filled with anger and resentment. The stories we choose to tell shape the emotions we feel and the relationships we build in the now.

That day became a turning point in our marriage. I committed even more deeply to letting go of my unhealthy beliefs, patterns, and stories. I chose to live from my updated operating system, to bring forward the assets of love, compassion, and truth, and to show up as my best self in our relationship.

Rewriting My Family Story with Love

My next step in healing my family story was to start telling a different story about my children.

For years, when people asked how they were doing, I would fall into a heavy, painful narrative and share about addiction, struggles, and all that was going wrong. But I began to realize that it was not my story to tell. It was also not helping me or them to keep repeating these painful recollections. Shifting the story did not mean pretending everything was fine or creating a fairytale. It meant being real, being honest, and choosing to answer from my Higher Self rather than from old wounds.

So when people asked, I started saying something like, "My kids are both in California. They're finding their way. They're learning to be self-supporting through their own contributions, and I'm really proud of them. Honestly, it's giving our family a lot of healing to have this space where we are each figuring out our own stuff. And when we do get time together, it feels even more special."

That was honest. That was expansive. It also allowed for more conversation if someone wanted to know more.

In this new season with my boys living in California, there were times, weeks or even months, when we had little communication. But I was learning to give them that space. I was letting them experience the cause and effect of their own choices. We were all beginning to live from a new way of being, one rooted in compassion and grace instead of control, entanglement and codependency

Most importantly, I was learning to see them as whole instead of broken. To see our family as whole instead of broken. That was the spiritually true story, the truth of our soul's journeys. That was the story I was determined to write because we cannot live from new principles if part of us is still sabotaging them by clinging to old pain and resentment.

By February, 2022, this shift had taken root so deeply that I could write in my journal:

> *I have come so far from the pain these pages hold... I am enough for me. I am not alone because I have me, and I am part of the whole of the Universe, and that is all I need.*

Transformation on Every Level

What I've learned over the years is that healing isn't a one-time event or a linear journey. Working the Recover Your Soul 9-Step Process has shown me that these steps are not something you finish. They continue to cycle and deepen over time. **Recovering Your Soul is an ongoing journey of healing and awakening, unfolding one layer at a time.**

It is a gift we are given to help us work through the complexity of being human. The protective layers of beliefs, stories, and patterns imprinted in our subconscious over a lifetime do not shift overnight. They take patience, willingness, and practice. But they do transform when we are ready to let go of control and see with a new perception.

And when they do, the transformation happens on every level.

Emotionally, we find ourselves responding differently to the old triggers. The anger doesn't grab us as tightly. The anxiety doesn't consume us. We have space to breathe, to choose, to witness our feelings without being overtaken by them.

Spiritually, we begin to trust something larger than ourselves. We release the illusion that we must manage and orchestrate everything alone. We remember our connection to Source and allow ourselves to be guided.

Intellectually, we start to question the stories we've been telling. We see our old beliefs for what they are and that they are simply protective patterns that once served us but no longer fit who we are becoming. We choose new thoughts and practice new ways of seeing.

And remarkably, science shows us that even our bodies, our very brain chemistry, begins to change.

I often use the analogy of computers to explain our beliefs as an operating system. Remember? The programs we run day after day, the code beneath it all that shapes how everything functions. When we practice new ways of thinking and being, we're not just changing a program. We're actually updating the operating system itself.

Our brains are designed to change. When we repeat old thoughts and patterns, we strengthen those pathways. They become automatic, like well-worn highways we travel without even thinking. For years, I had highways of "I'm not enough," "I must control everything," and "It's not safe to ask for what I need."

But when we choose new thoughts, when we practice new beliefs, when we respond from our Higher Self instead of our wounded self, we create new pathways. At first, they're rough and unfamiliar. The old highway still feels easier, more natural. But with practice, with patience, the new pathway strengthens.

And the old highway, no longer traveled, begins to fade.

This is why meditation works. Why prayer changes us. Why spiritual practice is called practice. We're literally retraining ourselves — not just spiritually, but physically. Our brain structure actually shifts with regular practice. The parts that handle fear and stress quiet down. The parts that support awareness, compassion, and connection grow stronger.

In awakening, we embrace new beliefs, creating new patterns. We learn to rewrite our story. We begin to change what we think, feel, and believe about the world. We see from a new perception. And from this empowered place, with Spirit as our co-creator, the possibilities become limitless.

This is why Recover Your Soul is a practice, not a destination. The operating system needs maintenance. New layers of understanding continue to reveal themselves. Each time we circle back through the steps, we go deeper. We see things we couldn't see before. We heal at levels we didn't know needed healing. **We are not who we were. We are remembering our wholeness, one choice at a time.**

Working the Steps in Your Own Life

Recover Your Soul - STEP 6

6. Embrace New Beliefs and Rewrite Your Story
Update Your Mindset: **Step into new beliefs and patterns that align with your Higher Self and expanded perception.** *Recognize Your Gifts:* **Acknowledge your unique gifts, assets, and strengths as you rewrite your personal story from a foundation of truth and love.**

***

This chapter has been about transformation — about the profound shift that happens when we choose to embrace new beliefs and rewrite the stories we've been telling about ourselves and our lives. For so long, I lived from outdated patterns, running programs of "not enough" and "must control." Those beliefs shaped everything.

Step 6 of the Recover Your Soul Process invites us to step fully into new ways of thinking, seeing, and living. **Embracing new beliefs is not about denying the past; it's about choosing to see it through the lens of wisdom, compassion, and growth, allowing those experiences to shape us into who we are becoming.**

When we update our beliefs and patterns to align with our Higher Self, transformation happens on every level, emotionally, spiritually, intellectually, and even physically. We begin to create from love and truth rather than from wounds and protection.

As we rewrite our personal stories, we honor the strengths, assets, and gifts that have always been within us. We see clearly the courage, resilience, and love that carried us to this moment. These are not new qualities we must develop. They were there all along, waiting to be remembered.

When you live from these updated beliefs, you remember the truth of who you are. You remember your wholeness. And you begin to live a story that reflects your authentic self and your connection with Spirit.

If you feel called to explore this step more deeply, I invite you to listen to these Recover Your Soul podcast episodes that share my own journey of rewriting old stories and stepping into new beliefs.

Podcasts About Embracing New Beliefs and Rewriting Your Story

https://recoveryoursoulbook.com/

Choosing a New Way to See

It is as I choose to see it – and I choose love. - RH

You have probably heard the phrase "aha moment." I prefer to call them moments of awakening. They are the moments when something shifts into place, one essential piece of the puzzle that suddenly lets you see the whole picture in a different light. A moment of awakening is a change in perception, a small recalibration in how you see and interact with the world.

As those little moments kept arriving for me, my entire view of life began to change. Things that used to feel fixed and immutable started to move. Patterns that had felt rigid loosened. Doors I had thought were closed opened just a little, and then a little more.

One of the most surprising awakenings was in my marriage. The husband I had spent so much time and energy trying to change and fix began to become my best friend. What I had written in my Prosperity Plus class vision about a partner I could laugh with, enjoy time with, and have a healthy relationship with was quietly unfolding.

He was still on his own healing and spiritual path, and his sobriety made a difference and was important. However, in many ways, he was the same man he had always been. What changed was me. I began to see him through a new lens of awareness. **When I stopped trying to control the story, the story between us softened and opened.**

The River Awakening

One of these moments of awakening came when Bodhi visited from California. He had stopped at a dispensary on the way to pick up a marijuana vape pen because he was not in one of his seasons of sobriety at that time.

Over the years, Rich and I had stopped trying to control their addictions, and we had an agreement that when they visited, they could be who they were. We only asked that they not get smashed at our house. They would smoke in the garage and have a few beers. Still, being sober around people who are not sober, especially your own children, is complicated even after doing so much work on detachment, spirituality, and Al-Anon. However, the more I learned not to focus on the substances, the more space I had to simply enjoy our time together and see them as they were, and that worked for me.

Rich and Bodhi loved to stand-up paddle on the rivers in Colorado, so we were driving to the nearest launch when Bodhi suddenly got anxious because he had left his weed pen behind. That set something off in Rich. He began to lecture Bodhi about his addiction and what he should be doing about it. Bodhi went defensive, and before long, they were arguing the way our family had argued for years. It was painful to watch. There I was, literally stuck between them in the front seat of my husband's truck.

This time I did something different. Instead of jumping in as I would have in the past, I used my new tools from Recover Your Soul and Al-Anon. I stayed out of it and simply sat with my own emotions.

It was uncomfortable, intense, and heartbreaking. My whole body felt tense.

It reminded me of the years of turmoil we had lived through with kids who were struggling and parents who did not know how to respond in the healthiest way.

In that moment, I recognized my own suffering in a fresh way. I closed my eyes and asked Spirit for help. I repeated that request as I slowed my breath. Then an inner answer came: "It is as I choose to see it." With that, I did not fall back into my old patterns of enabling, protecting, getting angry, or trying to fix things. I witnessed instead of intervening. I allowed both men to have their feelings. **I felt my sadness and discomfort without needing to change the situation.**

When we reached the river, the emotions were still high, so I walked away and gave them space. Rich took a walk of his own. Later, Bodhi came over and spoke with me. He opened up about what he was feeling, and I listened. I could be the loving mother I wanted to be without layering on the old habits of fixing or rescuing. I let him have his story. I let him be in all his feelings

I offered presence rather than solutions.

Eventually, Rich returned, and they talked things through. There were tears and hugs. They said things to one another that needed saying. In that moment, I saw something new: two people on their own paths, each with wounds that needed to be witnessed. I chose to see the scene as an opportunity for healing rather than as another damaging event.

I chose to see the family as capable of working through pain and coming out the other side with more repair than harm. **I chose to look through the eyes of love, and I saw more love.**

Choosing Love or Fear

The more I leaned into choosing this new perception, the stronger I became at staying present for myself and processing my feelings in healthy, empowered ways. It is a decision we make in each moment, yet when life gets messy, it can be so tempting to slip back into the old patterns and beliefs that are protecting our pain and discomfort.

We are always choosing between love and fear, expansion and contraction. I was learning that this work was not about being perfect or living up to some spiritual ideal that erases difficulty. Instead, it was about recognizing the invitation in every moment to choose to see love as the path forward. Those awakenings come in small moments, tiny shifts that add up into deep, lasting change.

I got better at letting go of control and trusting the intuition that was growing inside me. I found it easier to share my life from a place of authenticity and vulnerability, not only on the podcast but also with the people closest to me. I grew less afraid of what others might think. **I stopped defaulting to people-pleasing.**

Instead of putting everyone else first, I learned to check in with myself and notice when I was trying to control the outcome. I was also beginning to let others in to love me in a way that I had pushed away for so many years out of my fear and old limiting beliefs.

Christmas and Covid: A Test of New Patterns

I had an early taste of success with these new patterns when the boys came for our first Christmas together since they had moved away and after Covid in 2021. We were still early into our family recovery, with wins and crunchy moments both showing up, but overall, we were doing much better. One of our outings was to Meow Wolf in Denver, an immersive, interactive exhibition of art installations. My mom, who lives just a few miles away, came with us. We put on our masks and wandered through the exhibits together.

It was interesting to notice my old codependent tendency to make sure everyone else was having fun. Mostly, that meant making sure my sons were seeing and doing what they wanted. In doing so, I often distracted myself from truly appreciating the strange, beautiful art for its own sake.

Still, I could feel how far I had come. I was maybe 80 percent better than I had been before recovery. Just being aware of my hypervigilance was an improvement, and I used my relaxation and mindfulness tools to stay in the present moment and enjoy our time together as a family.

The next day on Christmas Eve, our church service was recorded and posted online, so my mom invited us to celebrate at her house. It was the first time in a long while we had all been there together, and it felt like a really lovely evening. I witnessed myself again being present instead of managing everyone else.

At the end of the night, we talked about Meow Wolf, and my mom asked the boys to join her for a full tour of her house. Bodhi happily obliged. Alex said he was too full from dinner and stayed on the couch. He had lived at her house and felt he knew it and all her treasures very well. I knew my mom would be disappointed, but I stayed out of it. I did not try to make everyone happy.

On Christmas morning, I woke up sick. We still had at-home Covid tests then, and mine was positive. I was disappointed. In my old life, that would have been a disaster. It was my job to take care of the family, especially at Christmas. Who would cook, clean up, keep the peace, and make sure everyone had what they needed? But in this new way of being, I let go of control. I quarantined and rested while the house carried on. I heard laughter, cooking, and the TV. They were fine without me.

I think that was the first time in my adult life that I allowed myself to be sick and actually enjoyed the permission to rest. It was a new gift to let others take care of me.

The Fire: Impermanence and Strength

Only a few days after the boys had gone back to California, on the first day I ventured out of my bedroom after Covid, the sky thickened with smoke, and we were told to evacuate. My mother filled her Subaru with what she could grab in the short time she had, and I could not help her because I was still contagious.

I did not think our homes were truly in danger, so I packed a few things and our important papers. Rich stayed with the house and shuttled our other cars and some possessions while I went to a friend's who also had Covid, and my mother evacuated to a friend's house. A few hours later, our entire town was on fire, and I watched it all unfold on my friend's laptop.

These are the moments when the new spiritual principles really come into play. Rich called to tell me he was staying in the neighborhood, putting out spot fires in the open space across from our house, and that his phone was almost out of battery, but he would be OK.

My mother called to say she had driven back into the area enough to see firsthand that her neighborhood was burning. I felt so helpless and so sad to imagine her beautiful house and her treasures lost.

And yet something inside me had shifted. I still felt the pain, and I shed the tears, but I did not fall into the old kind of suffering. If my mother's house had burned down, it was just as possible that our house would also be lost, but I had a new steadiness inside me.

I loved our home and our things, but I knew that our lives were the most valuable things of all. Not only our lives, but also the new life Rich and I had worked so hard to create, this new relationship in which I felt safe and excited for our next chapter. I trusted that together we could handle whatever came.

A few months before the fire, my mother and I had been on a walk. She turned a corner, looked at her house, and spoke about impermanence as she understands it in Buddhism. "This house," she said, "seems permanent, but you never know what may happen to it."

At the time, that idea seemed impossible, but she was right. She has been teaching those principles for decades. That night, her entire life burned to the ground.

Our house was saved, in part because Rich and the neighbor stayed up all night putting out embers in the open space across the street. I was deeply grateful to have our home, and the experience was another invitation to see my life through a new lens. I promised myself I would appreciate it more and not take my home and things for granted. At the same time, I could let them go, seeing them for what they are: material things that do not define the life I love.

My mother stood over the ashes of what had been her home and said, "Even through this, I choose to be happy."

Four years later, she lives in a lovely ranch even closer to me than the big house had been. She has created a beautiful life filled with art, treasures, and a quilting room. Through every difficult moment, she reminded me that we have the choice in how we see it and, in that choice, how we feel it. We choose the story we tell first to ourselves and then to the world.

Witnessing Rich and His Journey

Rich's path of recovering his soul has been very different from mine, and that is exactly as it should be. Each soul finds its way in its own timing. What matters is not that our journeys match, but that we continue to show up with honesty, willingness, and love. And I have watched Rich do that in a way that is deeply authentic to who he is.

When we quit drinking in 2018, Rich walked that early path with me. For the first three years of my sobriety, he was fully sober as well. We went to AA together, learning how to rebuild our marriage and our inner worlds together. Later, in his own timing, he stepped away from meetings and returned to an occasional drink, not as a collapse, but as part of his unfolding spiritual journey.

He never returned to daily drinking again luckily, and I no longer monitored his choices. By the time he decided on his own that drinking no longer had a place in his life, I had long released my attachment to his timetable, knowing I was powerless over it anyway.

My focus had become our spiritual path and the quiet changes I saw happening in his heart. That was what was most important to me.

And those changes were real. Over the years, Rich has softened in ways that still surprise me. A tenderness has emerged, a deep, steady kindness, that feels like a new language he learned by listening to his own soul. An outer reflection of who he was trying to be even in all those complicated years.

There have been challenges for him as he's aged: injuries, physical limitations, and the grief of no longer being "Superman" in the ways he once was. For someone who excelled at everything he touched, this has been humbling. But it has also been a profound teacher.

Through it, he has learned gentleness, patience, and self-love, spiritual tools he once resisted but now embraces in his own way.

And yes, he has used the teachings he picked up from me along the way. In the early days, when safety between us was still fragile, he couldn't tolerate hearing from "Rev. Rachel." But as healing continued and trust returned, something softened. He began coming to me with gratitude, naming the ways our lives had changed, acknowledging how much this journey had transformed him too and even asking for my coaching or views.

More and more, the two selves I once carried- Rachel and Rev. Rachel- are becoming one, and the same is true for him. We have both become more whole, more present, and more attuned. Two people who met as young adults are now growing older together with grace, laughter, and honesty.

Just as my Prosperity Plus vision had said all those years ago.

Indonesia: Seeing Each Other Through a New Lens

By the time we reached our 30th wedding anniversary, something in us had shifted so deeply that celebrating it felt like claiming a new chapter. We chose Indonesia - a bucket-list trip that symbolized everything we had worked for. Earlier in our marriage, I could not have pictured us traveling halfway around the world as the healthy, awake versions of ourselves that we are now.

Rich spent his days surfing, doing what he loves most, while I found myself under a palm tree meditating, journaling, and listening inward. And what struck me most wasn't the beauty of Indonesia, though it was stunning. It was the ease between us. The freedom. The tenderness.

Years ago, I would have molded myself around his needs, tracking every wave, making sure he was happy before even considering what I wanted. I would have erased myself without even realizing it.

But on this island in the Indian Ocean, everything was different.

I chose what nourished me.

He chose what nourished him.

And then we met in the middle at the end of each day, two souls aligned, sharing our joy, our stories, and the lightness we had created separately and together.

There was no hierarchy. No people-pleasing. No codependence. No hidden resentment.

Just two people, living their own truth, then returning to each other with open hearts.

This is what it feels like to align with a new perception.

To see one another through the eyes of the soul rather than the eyes of old wounds.

To love without control.

To walk together without walking the same.

Indonesia wasn't just a vacation. **It was the embodiment of who we had become, and that was partners who had recovered their souls both individually and together.**

A celebration of love that is free of codependency and pain. A marriage rooted in seeing through the eyes of love and forgiveness. A partnership guided by awakening and a daily choice to be 'in.'

Witnessing Bodhi and His Journey

When I think about Bodhi's journey, I'm reminded again and again of the practice of loving detachment and the gift of seeing with new eyes.

Looking back now, I can see something I couldn't see when we were living inside the storm: Bodhi had taken on the role of peacemaker in our family. It was the way he learned to survive, the way he created safety in a home filled with unspoken tension and unpredictable emotions. After that family therapy session where he finally shared his truth, that he had always felt left behind and invisible inside his own pain, both Rich and I made a conscious and tender effort to truly see him. Not the role. Not the mask. But the soul.

In college, Bodhi lived through a season of sobriety and found healing at Skate Church in Steamboat Springs. It was there he had a profound moment, hearing a voice tell him that if he continued down the destructive path he was on, he would lose everything he had dreamed of.

That experience planted a seed deep within him. Over the years, whenever I saw him drifting toward dangerous territory, I would gently remind him of that moment, hoping it would be an anchor he could return to.

But with time, I came to understand something essential:
His journey in and out of sobriety was never really about substances.

It was always about his *relationship with himself,* his spiritual path to self-worth and self-love.

The behaviors were symptoms.
The root was the pain of self-criticism, the belief that he had to earn his worth, the people-pleasing that kept him safe as a child, and the drive to succeed while secretly believing he was falling short.

Once I understood that, everything softened. I could finally let go with love.

There was a difficult season when Bodhi broke his collarbone at a Onewheel event, had surgery, and then re-broke it doing a backflip. He fell into a depression that frightened everyone around him. His identity was wrapped up in physical performance, and suddenly he couldn't show up the way he always had. Friends reached out, worried. He was afraid of losing everything he had built. And he lost sight of himself for a while.

The old me would have rushed in, tried to control, and tried to save him. But I had walked through the Recover Your Soul Process.

So instead, I checked in. I listened. I offered presence without solutions. I prayed. I sent love. And I practiced letting go.

His journey with sobriety continues. When he is sober, I feel the spark of hope that maybe he'll find his way earlier than I did. And when he returns to the old solution, I feel the ache of a mother's heart. **But now I can hold both the hope and the heartbreak without letting either define me.**

Bodhi has been on his own path for a long time now. His life looks nothing like the one I once imagined and everything like the one his soul came here to create. His passion for board sports, his creativity, his charisma, and his role as one of the originators of street style in the Onewheel community, he has built something authentic and uniquely his.

And something beautiful has happened in recent years.

Through his faith, his desire for awakening, and his own commitment to understanding himself, Bodhi has begun to see his challenges not as failures, but as opportunities to grow. He speaks openly now about the role he played in our family system, how being the peacemaker helped him survive as a child but also taught him to abandon himself.

He is actively working to release those people-pleasing beliefs and to show up in his life with more courage, more honesty, and more love for who he truly is.

Is his journey finished? Is he "fixed"? Absolutely not! And thank God I no longer need him to be.

He is still navigating his relationship with addiction. He is still healing old wounds. He is still learning how to stand in his true self, just as I am.

When I look at Bodhi now, I don't see brokenness. I see resilience. I see courage.
I see a soul asleep and awake, falling and getting back up, doing the work his soul came here to do.

I'm proud of him, not because he gets everything right, but because he keeps showing up with willingness. He follows the God of his own understanding, different from mine and uniquely his, and I respect him deeply for claiming his own path to faith.

And so when I witness Bodhi now, I see the light within him. I see the man he is becoming. And I choose to see his journey through the eyes of love. I choose to see him recovering his soul.

Letting Go of Alex

When Alex took that one-way flight to California, I felt both relief and terror in my body at the same time. After spending his entire life tracking his feelings, his choices, and his moods, trying to protect him from the heaviness he carried. It was strange to suddenly not have him right next to me. And yet, with the distance, a part of me could finally soften. I knew he was with Bodhi. I knew he was being cared for. I knew he was safe.

Still, it took years for the two of us to untangle the deep codependency we had woven together.

Alex had suffered from severe anxiety since he was a child that showed as panic from separation, deep depressive episodes, and self-harming thoughts that terrified me as a young mother. He'd been in therapy, spent time in a residential program, and gone to AA with me for a brief season after a DUI.

But therapy and medication had never felt like his path, and I understand that. As someone who used alcohol to manage my own pain, I know how easy it is to choose substances over feelings that feel too big to hold as a way to self-medicate.

He has gone through phases in his use, but sobriety and recovery is something he hasn't chosen, at least not yet.

Alex was always the one whose pain lived close to the surface. It made him the focus of our family for many years. But once he moved to California, fully on his own as an adult, I started to see him find his way...in his way.

I don't know everything about his inner world, because he doesn't share that part of himself with me. He isn't closed; he simply processes differently than I do and differently from Bodhi. But that doesn't mean he isn't learning what he came here to learn. His soul has its own curriculum.

At one point in my healing, I had a profound realization: Alex didn't come to me so I could fix or shape him. He came for my soul's journey so I could learn to love unconditionally, especially when loving felt hard, confusing, or painful. **He came through me because I could love him unconditionally enough to allow him to have all he needed to experience in his soul's journey.**

As the years in California unfolded, I began to see a man emerging, one who was healing in ways I could never have orchestrated. He started doing more of his art at the company he worked for. I could see the spark that had lived in him as a child, his vivid imagination and creativity coming back online. He began painting and creating graphics that carried his unique aesthetic: a blend of shadow, expression, and raw truth.

When he asked for a tattoo gun for his birthday, it didn't surprise me. It became another channel for his creativity. Both he and Bodhi now carry his art on their bodies, literal expressions of connection and legacy.

Alex and Rich are still finding their way with each other. Once I stepped back and released my ideas of how their relationship "should" be, they began to navigate it themselves. Creativity became the place where they could meet without pressure or expectation.

There was a moment, early on in those California years, that marked a turning point for me. I was visiting and worrying, falling back into old patterns. Alex gently stopped me, took my hands, looked straight into my eyes, and said, "Mom, you don't have to worry about me anymore. I've got this. I'm going to be okay."

I burst into tears. Twenty years of fear released in a single breath. He wasn't promising an easy road, but I could feel the truth of what he said. It was time to truly let go.

Three years into his move, he met his soulmate, a woman who loves him with a steadiness and acceptance that has helped him heal pieces of himself I could never reach. I've never seen him so settled in who he is.

And in February of 2025, they welcomed a baby boy into the world, our first grandchild.

Is it perfect? No. It is beautifully real, just like my own marriage, my own parenting, and my own healing. But I see the depth of their love. I see their dedication. I see Spirit holding all three of them as they navigate this new chapter.

During the baby's first year, we had more visits than we'd had in a long time. It has been such a gift to meet each other again, not as the roles we once played, but simply as the souls we are today. **This is what unconditional love looks like. Seeing the light in my son, even when the path is messy or unclear. Choosing unconditional love.**

Living Fully Awake

When we step fully into our lives, being present in each moment, whatever it is, we step fully into this journey of our soul.

Over the last eight years, I have become more aware of the preciousness of our one life in this incarnation.

Choosing to be awakened has actually opened my heart up to a deeper level of feelings than I ever allowed myself to feel before, because I was so protected and distracted with controlling them. I have witnessed myself wanting to fall into fearful patterns when a trigger appears, but I now see that these are actually opportunities to grow and deepen my awakening experience and to heal on a new level.

Being conscious and awake, especially during complex and challenging moments, means that you are showing up for yourself as your authentic Higher Self. This is who my soul is calling me to be in my own life. I can now see the many moments of awakening that were there for me, even when I couldn't see them in the hard years.

I never want to diminish the real challenges our family faced during those years, but I now have a different perspective on it and a different way of looking at it. An awakened perception.

We have albums filled with pictures of us laughing and having fun. Those are real moments and were as true as the times that were painful. We went on trips and adventures, and Rich and I loved our children more than anything, and it shows in those albums.

My journals may speak of my own journey of pain, and those words are their own moments and how it felt to me and a way I saw it in those moments of anguish. They are valid, but they do not have to be the way I continue to remember and tell the story of my life and our family's life.

Time and healing are amazing things, as all that really exists is this present moment in time. In this moment, I can choose to be awake and conscious. In this moment, I can honor how I feel and trust that I have the spiritual tools of love to allow what is happening in this moment, whether it is easy or complex.

As I grow older, I am also aware of how precious and fleeting time is, and I don't want to waste it by living those old stories and patterns. I want to fully engage in this spiritual path and live a happy and healthy life. **It is as I choose to see it – and I choose love.**

Working the Steps in Your Own Life

Recover Your Soul - STEP 7

7. Align with a New Perception
Shift Your Perception: **Align with a new, healthier perception of yourself and the world around you.** *Choose Your Reality:* **Consciously shape your experience by aligning thought, word, and action with your awakened perception and Higher Self.**

***

This chapter has been about alignment, about learning to see ourselves and the world through the eyes of our Higher Self rather than through the lens of our wounded self. There is a spiritual truth that says we don't get what we want; we get who we are. For so long, I tried to change everything outside of me, hoping it would finally make me happy. What I discovered is that transformation comes from aligning with my soul's true nature.

Step 7 of the Recover Your Soul Process invites us to shift our perception and align with a new, healthier way of seeing ourselves and the world around us. This is about choosing to see through the eyes of love, compassion, faith, and forgiveness. When we do this, all judgment falls away. We become present with and able to allow all that is.

What changes is not the circumstances, but who we are in relationship to them. We begin to consciously shape our experience by aligning our thoughts, words, and actions with our awakened perception and Higher Self. We stop waiting for the world to change and instead become the change we've been seeking.

Each moment offers us a choice: Will I see this through the eyes of fear or the eyes of love? Will I respond from my wounds or from my wholeness? The more we choose to align with our Higher Self, the more our reality shifts to reflect that alignment. We become who we truly are, and from that place, everything transforms.

This is not perfection – it is presence. It's the ongoing practice of returning to love, releasing judgment, and allowing ourselves to be guided by our soul's wisdom rather than our fear.

If you feel called to explore this step more deeply, I invite you to listen to these Recover Your Soul podcast episodes, where I share stories, tools, and practices that support aligning with new perceptions and choosing to see through the eyes of your Higher Self.

Podcasts About Aligning with a New Perception

https://recoveryoursoulbook.com/

CHAPTER 9:
A Spiritual Practice

Spirituality isn't something that I do. It's how I see. - RH

The morning is my favorite part of my day. I wake with the sun and the stillness of a new day. I light incense and a candle, meditate, read a passage from a spiritual book, and journal while new age music plays softly in the background. This is when I feel most at home in myself and most in connection with all that is.

Even after my formal practice concludes, the morning remains a sacred thread throughout my day. I listen to spiritual or educational books and podcasts while getting ready or doing chores, carrying that calm with me into the ordinary moments.

Being raised by a Buddhist mother, you might think this would have come naturally, but for a long time it did not. I remember seasons of chaos when I felt overwhelmed, and my mother would gently say, "You do not have to sit for an hour or even for half an hour. Just close your eyes and be still for five minutes."

At the time, I did not believe I could carve out even five minutes from all that needed fixing, changing, or controlling. I did not understand how those five minutes could make a difference.

Now I often give myself an hour or two, sometimes three if the day allows, to settle into a place beyond the everyday. It is a place beyond the chaos, a still and quiet space where I remember my wholeness and connection to Spirit. It is where wisdom arises, insight shows up, guidance appears, and peace rests in me.

The Foundation of Morning Practice

I am so grateful this practice took root while I was studying to become a minister. It has become a ritual I hold with reverence, not only for the peace it brings and the study it allows, but also for the power of setting an intention for the day. Abraham Hicks calls this "calibrating." When we open to that spiritual space in the morning, we set the vibration, the energy, the intention, the calibration for the day. By writing even a few lines of gratitude or intention each morning along with meditation and study, I feel the shift that comes from beginning the day on purpose.

Over time, I noticed that how my day unfolded had its foundation in my morning routine. If I woke up, skipped my practice, and went straight to my phone to check email, social media, or the news, the day rarely moved as smoothly as it did when I started with spiritual practice, however long or short.

Today, the invitation to spiritual practice is more common than ever. Apps, videos, books, playlists, classes, retreats, and even workplace programs make it easier to find a practice that fits. The language around meditation, mindfulness, metaphysics, and mystical teaching is not nearly as fringe as it was even 10 years ago. There is a collective shift happening, a change in our collective consciousness some call the Great Awakening.

This is not about one person being better than another or anyone being chosen over others. We are each here on our own soul journey in what is often called Earth School. We each have our own curriculum of experience, healing, and awakening. It is not a competition. It is not a judgment that someone who meditates for five hours a day is better than someone who sits for five minutes or even not at all. The practice is the practice, and what matters is that you show up for yourself.

Coming Home to Ourselves

This is really about coming back to ourselves, about deepening our connection to soul and spirit, and about choosing to be awake. It means releasing the urge to compare our journey to anyone else's and staying focused on our own healing. It means fully letting go of judgment, first of ourselves and then of what we see around us. **True transformation is on an energetic level beyond the analysis of every memory or wound.**

It is a profound opening to witness the wholeness we are as souls and allow the wounds and judgments to fall away and come home to love.

It is remembering that we are powerless over everything outside ourselves, and how that is actually freedom from the suffering and fear that come from trying to control what is. It is taking our power back and putting our focus on our spiritual connection as our priority and source of joy.

When I first got sober, I stopped watching the news as part of my spiritual practice, and Rich graciously went along with that choice. I could feel how the news generated tension and how it was curated around fear.

This was not about sticking my head in the sand. It was about deciding what I would allow to occupy space in my mind. I already had enough real work to do with my own family without inviting a whole world of chaos into my daily thoughts.

Of course, there is no complete escape from news unless you leave society entirely, but you can decide whether you will consciously let it be part of your intake.

At first, I worried I might be missing out, or that skipping the news meant I was uncaring. But the more I studied spiritually, the more I heard teachers advising caution about what we feed our minds. Many recommend avoiding violent and aggressive media or entertainment of any kind. We become what we consume, so choose what aligns with how you want to feel.

When I listened to Dr. Wayne Dyer on the Tao, I heard similar guidance: Avoid anger and violence not only in action but in thought. Limiting sensationalist news has given me space to heal my nervous system and feel more at ease.

The same is true for entertainment. Rich and I still enjoy an hour or two of TV most nights, but I have become very selective about what I watch. I used to watch intense dramas full of violence because that was what Rich was watching.

Now I am drawn to nature documentaries, uplifting competition shows like Project Runway or the Great British Baking Show, documentaries about the beautiful spirit of humans, spiritual and mystical programs, or anything light-hearted, and Rich has obliged (although he still watches his style of shows without me). As a child, I relied on TV as a steady companion, and in many ways, it has continued to serve that role for me as an adult, still a reliable friend.

Today, the need TV once filled has changed. My spiritual practice now gives me that steadiness and a feeling of connection that allows me to never feel lonely, and I use that time to listen to or watch what fills me up rather than to hide or numb.

The Power of Curated Consciousness

This daily practice of calibrating my life through journaling, morning spiritual rituals, and carefully curating what I allow into my mind and what I listen to, watch, or read has been an anchor I can't overstate.

It has carried me through the storms of the last eight years: the upheaval of changing jobs again and again, the ache of watching my children wrestle with addiction, sometimes slipping deeper into it, finding stretches of fragile sobriety, sometimes shining beautifully in minor seasons of clarity only to fall back to the old solution of addiction. Through life with Rich as he continued to battle his own demon of addiction and midlife crisis.

Through it all, I have grown in my ability to detach with love, to hold my family in compassion without losing myself in their chaos or choices.

Gratitude has become the cornerstone of this practice. By choosing to see what I am thankful for, I shift my focus from what is missing or painful to what is good and sustaining. Every morning, I begin my journal with the same words:

"Thank you, Spirit, for my precious and beautiful life."

That simple opening creates space for my journal to become more than a record of often difficult events. It becomes a conversation with Spirit, with my Higher Self, a safe place to process the complexity of my feelings.

When I reviewed my journals in preparation for this book, I realized how deeply they have marked my healing. The early pages are heavy with raw pain, full of the voice of who I was then, desperate to put my grief and anger somewhere. But over time, those same journals, once pages of pain, transformed into dialogues filled with guidance, love, and a higher perspective, a new perception.

In February of 2022, I wrote:

> *Coming back to the book of pain, old, familiar feelings and patterns of loneliness, sadness, doubt, and fear; wanting to let them go, but they cling to me like ash. Drop your sword and come off the battlefield. Release your unrealistic expectations of yourself and others. Allow him to be exactly who he is and accept and appreciate the beauty of it all.*

Only a few years into sobriety and a spiritual journey, I was no longer drowning in pain. I was witnessing it. I could hold it, process it, and then choose to release it. Later in that entry, I wrote:

> *I have come so far from the pain these pages hold, and yet there is still a place where my pain is deep. No one else is going to heal that pain. I am my own best friend. I am the only one who can choose to feel happy and loved.*

The shift was profound. Journaling stopped being about documenting my suffering and became a sacred mirror, one that showed me both where I had been and who I was becoming.

Opening to Deeper Guidance

A few years ago, I had one of those moments of awakening while listening to my friend's podcast, *Breath In, Breath Out,* by Krystal Jakowsky. She was interviewing someone who was reading her Akashic Records.

It was a concept I had heard before but never really understood.

At the next red light, curiosity got the best of me. I grabbed my Audible app, searched, and before the light turned green, I had bought the first thing that popped up. What I didn't realize until later was that it wasn't an audiobook. It was actually a course by Linda Howe on how to read the Akashic Records.

Like so many of the glimmers that the Universe has placed along my path, this felt like the exact right thing at the right time.

By then, I had already been offering spiritual coaching, sharing the Recover Your Soul Process that continued to unfold as I worked with more clients. From the very first session, I felt inner guidance to begin with a grounding meditation, something no one had ever done for me in the counseling I had received. Yet, when I trusted that nudge, I could feel the power of centering both myself and my client before diving in.

The surprising part was that the less I thought about what I should say in that meditation, the more the words flowed through me. Sometimes what came out connected directly to what the client later shared in session. Other times, a client would stop and say, "I can't believe you said that because..." and then reveal something deeply personal.

Even when old fears tried to whisper that I should play it safe, I knew the truth: These words weren't coming from me alone. They were coming through me. I was channeling the guidance from somewhere beyond me.

That's when the Akashic Records course entered my life. It provided me with the language, tools, and structure to deepen the channel I was already experiencing. I began incorporating the Records into my personal journals, asking for guidance on my soul's journey. Through automatic writing, I started receiving messages that were profoundly loving and healing, helping me release old pain and take a step further into trust.

Soon, this guidance began flowing in sessions with clients as well. It didn't feel like I was "fixing" them, but rather holding space for their wholeness and sharing what came through. When I trusted and shared the messages, sessions unfolded with more clarity and ease, as though we were being guided together.

As time passes, I am more and more comfortable with this guidance that flows through me, and I am not afraid to name myself as a channel.

I also carried this trust into my speaking. After leaving my job at the church, opportunities opened for me to speak at Unity and various spiritual centers a few times each month. Initially, I spent hours preparing and researching the material. I would outline my key points and choose the full flow of the talk.

But over the years, I noticed something: When I opened myself completely and allowed the words to flow, the talks carried more power. The stories of my own experience, woven with teachings that had shaped me, felt more authentic when I trusted the channel instead of the script.

Now, I still prepare. I continue to research and reflect on the message I want to bring. But I do it lightly, leaving space for Spirit to move through me. And the more I trust that flow, the clearer and more impactful the message becomes.

Trusting My Own Experience

I have always believed, and still feel, that we all have access to divine and infinite wisdom. Yet for a long time, my old limiting beliefs tried to hold me back in fear. I hesitated to claim the experiences I was having. Instead, I compared myself to other healers and teachers, those who could see auras, channel direct messages from guides they could see, connect with souls on the other side, or read the Akashic Records with details of past lives.

Those comparisons only deepened my fear of rejection and my old wound of not being enough. My Higher Self knew the truth: Comparison only leads to suffering. By thinking I needed to do it "better," or in some way that looked like someone else's path, I was blocking myself from deepening into what was already opening for me.

I realized that I didn't need to name it, and it didn't need to resemble anyone else's experience. Spiritual connection is not one-size-fits-all. It is unique, intimate, and personal. My role was not to replicate someone else's gifts but to honor my own.

I have always been a broad-stroke person. I think and feel in pictures and emotions rather than in exact details. I don't always remember conversations, books, or movies word for word, but I remember how they made me feel. And now, in this trusting place, awake in the present moment, I discovered something remarkable: peace and love were already here.

I began to understand the incredible gift of feelings. For most of my life, I hadn't trusted mine. Instead, I worked to control the world around me, trying to change my outer circumstances so I wouldn't have to feel uncomfortable inside. But feelings are not meant to be controlled or avoided. They are guides pointing the way to peace.

Even now, when my mind starts to chatter or control sneaks in, I remind myself, "All is well." From that grounded space, I can witness what is happening around me without the frantic urge to fix it. I see more clearly that the harder I try to control everything, the more uncontrollable it becomes. Instead, I allow my feelings to move through me, trusting the truth from the rooms of recovery: "This too shall pass."

As I release and allow, the guidance that once only came through journaling or in sessions now flows into my everyday life. I notice it in my coaching, in my speaking, and in my relationships. The more I trust, the more I see; big changes are happening, and they begin within me.

Healing My Marriage through Presence

It has helped me heal my marriage. In this space, I am able to be present with my husband in a way I never could before, because I have stopped trying to fix him. I have stopped trying to change him. Now I see a person, a man, a soul in front of me who feels very different from the one I used to experience.

Together, we have created a way of life that is gentle and kind, filled with laughter and ease. I can now have hard conversations because I feel the presence of my Higher Self with me.

We often remark that it is as if we are completely different people. Not leaving behind who we were, but we have become more true to our authentic selves. Without the layers of protection, fear, and old belief systems, and without reacting from our character defects, our true nature has space to shine. And that true nature is kindness and heart. From this place, we have created a deep sense of safety in our relationship.

I can look back at my old journals, filled with complaints and frustrations, and smile. The unfinished house projects, the piles of his stuff, the laundry left undone, and the dishes that never seem to make it from the sink to the dishwasher. All of those things are still here. But they no longer bother me like they did before.

I have had people say that they want to stay in their marriage because of the choices I made. I am quick to respond that we are each walking our own path and must look honestly and deeply at what is right for ourselves and not stay just because I made that choice.

I have had clients say that they wanted to follow the Al-Anon principles well enough that they could stay in a relationship, even though their partner was still drinking or not choosing to be healthy or awake. Although there is truth in the practice of being in presence, and we can learn to accept in ways that can give us strength in complex relationships, we must never abandon ourselves or settle for what is not healthy for us. **It is not about judgment but about alignment.**

I have stayed because my marriage continues to be a safe place for me to deepen my spiritual practice and awaken to myself. If a day comes where I no longer feel safe or that I am abandoning myself, I may make a different choice. **It is in our relationships that we have some of the greatest opportunities for spiritual growth and awakening.**

In my journal entry in May of 2022, I found myself wrestling with old patterns, but I had tools to approach them differently. I wrote:

> *Can I let him be to think and act in ways that upset me? Let him do all the things he wants to do, and I'll just be me. That means I'll feel sad and lonely sometimes. and that's OK. I can sit with it. I see now that the frustration I feel is really just sadness underneath. And I hand that sadness over to God.*

Those words offered evidence of a shift happening within me. The old triggers did not hit me in the same way. I was moving into a new way of being. In this same space, I found the ability to witness what was happening in the lives of others, including Rich, with compassion. Instead of trying to control or correct, I could simply witness the complexity of being human.

Mostly, I let go of the part of me that believed I knew better. I began to trust that there is always more happening than I can understand, that we are all woven into the great web of Universal flow. Life is not punishment or reward. Our souls are here to have complex experiences, and when we allow ourselves to move with the flow, we can let go of our resistance and suffering, and we experience freedom.

By January, 2023, I write in my journal, noting that I could see the integration of this practice in even the smallest moments of relationship tension. I wrote:

> *I accept Rich as he is. I also accept and feel the awareness*
> *that he cannot be and give me all I need and want. I release, I*
> *release, I allow.*

These simple words represented years of spiritual work distilled into practice: the ability to love without needing to change, to accept without becoming bitter, to release without abandoning love, but mostly without abandoning myself.

I have released many of our roles. Rich and I joke that our couples counseling is paying someone to come clean the house, because it supports our relationship and is much better than me silently resenting the chores. Sometimes I cook, sometimes he cooks. And no one keeps score. That, for me, is freedom.

I had written many songs about the complexity and heartbreak of life, but it was in the pandemic that I finally wrote a love song for Rich that shared with simplicity the journey we had been on together.

"I Fell for You" by Rachel Harrison

https://www.recoveryoursoul.net/music

Living in Divine Flow

And this daily practice, this choice to prioritize my spiritual life, has meant that things began working out in profound ways that are hard to explain. **What I've discovered, and what you may too, is that when you truly trust the Universe, Spirit, God, Source, or whatever name you give it, life begins to unfold naturally, beautifully, and often with a touch of surprise.**

One of the most unexpected changes has been my relationship with time. I used to feel like I was always running behind, never with enough hours in the day, overwhelmed by what I couldn't get done. Now it feels as though time works in my favor instead of against me.

I trust that things will work out, and rather than forcing or pushing, I listen to my inner guidance. This has created space, real space, in every part of my life.

It has also opened the door for what some might call coincidences, but I believe are Spirit-driven synchronicities, such as happened one quiet Sunday morning. Rich and I were sipping coffee on the couch when I felt a nudge, an inner whisper: Go try out that new restaurant down the street for breakfast.

I turned to Rich and said, "Hey, let's go there for breakfast." He looked at me with surprise because spontaneity, especially without getting ready first, has never been my style. But we went. And halfway through our meal, his older brother walked in. He lives in the same town, but they hadn't connected for a long time. In that moment, I knew this wasn't random. It was a gentle and beautiful opening for them to reconnect, simple, ordinary, yet deeply meaningful.

Moments like that happen again and again. A nudge to go to the grocery store, and there's the person I needed to see or the one item I'd been hunting for, suddenly back in stock. A nudge to turn down a side street, and I stumble on a garage sale with just the thing I didn't even know I was looking for. **The more I listen, the more I notice. The more I trust, the more I see how the Universe is always reminding me that there is enough of everything for everyone.**

When I stay clear in my own energy and remain present in the moment, I can hear that guidance more easily. And when I follow it, I find myself in the flow, living proof that Spirit's invitations often come as small whispers that turn into profound blessings.

Winters at the Beach

I still remember sitting in Prosperity Plus, writing out my vision of the life I longed for. One line was so clear: winters at the beach. At the time, it felt like a fantasy. How could I, an office manager struggling to make ends meet, ever make that happen?

And yet it has. It may not be the whole winter, but every year since, Rich and I have found our way to the ocean for at least a few weeks. Those trips are a touchstone for me, a reminder that Spirit was listening, that co-creation is real, and that what we write with clarity and intention has a way of finding us. I feel so lucky and grateful every time I look out on the ocean, knowing that it is so much more than a vacation or destination. **It is a reminder that it is okay to want and ask the Universe, and to receive.**

Strength for All of Life's Experiences

This awakened and connected way of being also gives me strength when life is hard. It steadies me through heartbreak or sadness, through painful conversations and feelings. Because that too is part of the spiritual journey, to know sorrow as well as joy, to allow pain as much as love.

It isn't all bliss, rainbows, and butterflies. It is about living fully, deeply, and openly with *everything* life brings. It is about remembering that we are connected to absolutely everything and realizing that how we choose to see it will shape how it feels for us.

I feel as though I am seeing the world with new eyes. It is as if a fog has lifted, and I can finally take in the miracles that are right in front of me in every moment. In the summer, I enjoy sitting in our backyard and simply observing nature. The squirrels darting across branches, the butterflies floating on the air, the bees moving from flower to flower, the birds singing, and the plants slowly reaching for the sun.

I watch them as though I were a child seeing them for the very first time.

Something remarkable happens in that space of trust. I no longer take any of it for granted. The complexity, intricacy, and majesty of it all moves me. Out of a seed so small emerges a plant that becomes leaves, blossoms, fruit, vegetables, food for us, food for animals, and nectar for bees.

Everything works together. And we, too, are part of that same miracle. Our souls have come here on purpose to experience all of it.

This spiritual journey is not about escaping what is hard. It is about being fully present to the gift of life, even when it feels uncertain or messy. It is about trusting that things will ultimately work out, though not always in the way we first imagined.

When we listen to our intuition and honor our feelings, we are guided toward what our souls came here to experience and learn from.

And when we let go, when we allow that flow, we often discover more than we ever could have dreamed for ourselves and fully step into the unlimited potential of what our souls can be in this lifetime in an awakened state

Spiritual Practice Comes First

What I have found is that if I do not prioritize my spiritual practice, it becomes very easy to slip back into irritation, frustration, and the old urge to control. The moment I start believing I can manage things on my own, without listening to intuition or asking to be of service, life begins to feel hard and overwhelming again.

After all these years, I still try to remember the prayer from AA's Step Three every morning before I get out of bed and every night before I fall asleep, just as my sponsor once taught me.

On days I forget, I may simply say, "Thank you for my precious life. Lead me where you need me. I am so grateful. Namaste." Even that small moment of intention brings me back to the present and reminds me that the only thing I can truly control is myself, to choose love, and to be of service.

Allowing the Universe to be my source and guide has become something like a joyful game. I find myself curious, wondering what Spirit will bring me next. It often feels like receiving gifts: the next book, the next teaching, the next nudge of wisdom to study or listen to. Each person's journey of awakening is unique, and what sparks one heart may not speak to another. That's the beauty of it.

For me, the path has led deeper into the teachings of the mystics and metaphysics. Again and again, I find that what I am reading aligns with the words I have already written in my journals through automatic writing or exploring the Akashic Records in meditation. It feels as though each new level builds upon the last, fitting puzzle pieces into place more quickly, even as the puzzle itself keeps growing.

And the deeper I go, the more I see how vast it all is. The more I learn, the more I realize how little I know. But that realization no longer frightens me. I don't need to be an expert or have it all figured out. My role is simply to stay open, to gather the broad strokes, to listen for the next right step on my journey, and to let my soul lead the way.

All Paths Lead to Love

It has strengthened my trust that I am on the right path *for me*, and it has opened my heart to see that beneath every religion and spiritual tradition there is a shared essence of love. I can now listen to perspectives very different from my own, even those that speak in absolutes or offer certainty through fear, without being pulled into the anxiety or division that used to upset me.

Instead, I look past the surface layers and listen for the Universal Truth underneath it all, the thread of love that I believe is the true intention of every teaching.

I practice seeing wholeness in the people I love and then expand that practice outward, even to those whose views of the world feel opposite from mine. I no longer want to feed the division that is so often reinforced in our country and our world, because division only fuels fear.

I may not agree with everything I see or hear, but my spiritual tools remind me that *nothing* is truly unacceptable. There is Source, there is God, in everything, especially in what I do not yet understand.

Over the past eight years, I have stepped into a completely different life than the one I used to see and experience. Not that my old life was wrong or bad, but it simply no longer worked for me. I am deeply grateful to have entered this new and peaceful way of living, supported by a tribe of spiritual sisters and friends with whom I can have wild and deep conversations, where I can show up exactly as I am. There is no need to please, nor is there a need to conform.

I am especially grateful for the *Recover Your Soul* community that has formed around me, which gives me strength every single day to stay grounded and continue on this healing path. I have learned that the only way I can truly serve my family, community, and the wider world is to stay focused on my own spiritual journey, to embody the principles I am learning, and to continue to learn, heal, and awaken.

At times, it is still hard to leave the safe bubble of peace I've created in my home. But I am no longer ruled by level-nine anxiety that once pushed me to take care of everything and everyone. I don't want to lose the part of myself that is skilled at organizing and caring and can get things done, but now I can bring those gifts from a place of wholeness and not from the old codependent self that believed it was my job to fix the world.

Connected to my Higher Self, I can show up in my fullness and with an open heart. I trust that I have what it takes to be present for whatever comes, both the beautiful and the difficult. **I see love in everything** when I choose to see through the eyes of love. Even when love doesn't seem to be what I am looking at, I can always choose love.

Working The Steps in Your Own Life

Recover Your Soul - STEP 8

8. Deepen Your Spiritual Practice
Commit to Presence: **Develop regular spiritual practices that keep you grounded in the present and connected to your Higher Self and the Higher Power of your understanding.** *Live in Alignment:* **Continue to release old stories and embody the principles of Recover Your Soul as a daily way of being.**

***

Deepening your spiritual practice is not about perfection or escape; it's about presence, growth and transformation. It is about awareness and staying conscious. It is about choosing, day after day, to return to your center, to listen to your intuition, and to walk as your Higher Self in partnership with a Higher Power and honoring the journey of your soul.

Through this practice, the ordinary becomes sacred: a journal page, a quiet prayer before sleep, a conversation with a loved one, or even the simple act of noticing the world around you. Over time, you realize that your spiritual practice is not something you fit into life. It becomes the way you live your life and who you are. This path will not always be easy. You will still face challenges, heartbreak, and uncertainty. But when you are grounded in your spiritual practice, and you meet those moments with compassion, strength, and trust. You learn to let go of control, to see through the eyes of love, and to flow with the wisdom of the Universe.

Your journey to Recover Your Soul is uniquely yours, yet you are never alone in it. We are all part of the same great web, each of us learning, growing, and returning to love in our own way.

I choose to deepen my practice. I choose to live from my Higher Self. I choose love.

If you'd like ongoing support on this journey, I invite you to listen to these episodes from the *Recover Your Soul* podcast, where we explore these practices more deeply together.

Podcasts to Deepen Your Spiritual Practice

https://recoveryoursoulbook.com/

CHAPTER 10:
Shine Your Light

Shining our light does not mean that we save everyone.
It means we illuminate the path if they so choose to walk
it. - RH

About 20 years ago, I was introduced to the Enneagram, a system of nine personality archetypes that helps us understand both our own patterns and the motivations of others. It was a game-changer for me. I discovered that I was a Peacemaker. My well-being depended on others being OK, and if they were not, I felt compelled to make things right.

Learning the Enneagram also opened my eyes to the personalities of my family members. It gave us a common language and some tools to understand better where each of us was coming from and what made us feel safe, happy, or uncomfortable.

At the time, however, I took the label of Peacemaker very literally. I believed it was my responsibility to fix things for everyone in my life. If someone was unhappy, unsettled, or uncomfortable, I thought it was my job to smooth it over, to change the situation, to make it better.

Through my journey of awakening and recovering my soul, I have come to a different understanding. My role is not to make peace for others but to make peace within myself. **True peace is not about changing what is happening around me, but about showing up as a presence of peace in the midst of it.**

Now I see that being a Peacemaker is not about control; it is about being, simply being. It is choosing to embody peace as a way of living, rather than trying to manufacture it for others.

Understanding Light

One of the spiritual principles that has become clearer to me is the concept of light and the energy it represents. The deeper I went into spirituality, the more I noticed the word "light" everywhere. What is this light? Light is energy. It is there at the very beginning of the Bible: "Let there be light" (Genesis 1:3). With those words, light appeared and separated from darkness.

Light brings illumination. And I have learned in my Recover Your Soul journey that the darkness is not bad. Darkness is not wrong. It is an essential element of the Universe, just as in the polarity of yin and yang in Eastern philosophy. The contrast and polarity are essential for creation.

Light does not erase the dark; it reveals what is hidden. When we bring light to a situation, we offer illumination, but we cannot force anyone else to see it. Each person must choose their own light. Our task is not to control or create another's experience. Our task is to tend to our own. To shine our own light. To be a peacemaker within our own being. To cultivate and protect the light within us.

I now understand that the most significant impact we can have is through our demonstration and walking our talk. When I recognized that I was powerless over people, circumstances, and outcomes, I discovered freedom. Letting go allowed me to trust that others are on their own path and have their own unique experiences. What I can influence is my own path, my own choices, and my own experience.

That shift was powerful. I was taking my power back. I was learning to be at peace even when those around me were not. And I could do this without shrinking myself, without people-pleasing, and without the old patterns of codependency. I no longer needed to play small. I could simply shine.

The Power of Authentic Presence

It meant that I could bring my authentic self into every conversation, every situation, and every encounter. There is an opportunity in every thought I think and every word I speak to embody higher consciousness, to speak of love, to live with authenticity, and to show up strong and grounded in each interaction.

This, to me, is the true power of shining my light. Not to change others, but because shining is what we are here to do. And when we are around people who are struggling, and we all have someone in our lives who is struggling, we begin to see that we cannot and should not force anyone to change.

You cannot make someone choose light if they are in the darkness. And there is value in the darkness. For a long time, I could not understand that. I resisted it. But now I see that my time in darkness and suffering shaped me into who I am today. Those experiences, just as they were, became part of the gift.

Looking back, I see a lifetime woven with joys and sorrows, addiction and healing, clarity and awakening, despair and grace. All of it, every single moment, was an important part of the process. And now I can feel gratitude for it all.

I was 48 years old when I finally made the decision to stop drinking. Others had tried to help me, had pleaded with me to heal, but only I could choose when I was ready. I was 48 years old when I finally chose to stop codependently caregiving and fixing everything and everyone around me in unhealthy ways.

I had heard the messages, read the books, and attended church and classes. But transformation did not come until the pain of staying in the bud was greater than the fear of blooming.

If that was true for me, can I not extend the same grace to others? Can I sit with people as they are instead of trying to fix or change them? Can I let my own healing be the example? Because the greatest gift we can ever give anyone is to do our own healing and to walk into each situation with compassion, kindness, forgiveness, and grace. To accept and unconditionally love people as they are.

Acceptance does not mean agreement. It does not imply approval. It means no longer wasting energy trying to force change where it cannot be forced. You cannot change the weather, nor can you change the people in your life. We cannot make people want to change or even heal themselves.

This, to me, is what it means to be a Peacemaker, not in the world outside, but within my own heart and soul.

Grace in Relationships

This grace continues to heal the relationships in my life. It allows me to love and accept my husband for who he is, to be in our marriage for who we are today, rather than living from the pain of the past. It allows me to release my children to live their lives as they choose, trusting that their journey is their own. It even softens how I engage with the world, freeing me from being overly invested in politics or clinging tightly to one side.

Grace has also taught me that there are many ways to show up in life. All of them are valid, and there is no single right or wrong way. I no longer need to be the one who knows it all. Sometimes the wisest response is to remain quiet. To listen. To let go of the need to share an opinion or to prove a point.

As I began to live this way, I noticed my friendships shifting. The people I once drank with, complained with, or bonded with over old patterns began to fall away. Not because anything was wrong with those friendships, but because they no longer aligned with who I was becoming. I asked Spirit for a new tribe, friends who could meet me in this new space of authenticity and awakening. Slowly, beautifully, they appeared.

And when I find myself in solitude, it no longer feels lonely. It feels whole and nourishing. I have learned when to say yes and when to say no. I am content because when I do choose to show up, I show up freely, not out of obligation or expectation. I show up not to change anything, but simply to shine my light. To be a presence of acceptance and care. To meet people exactly where they are, without judgment.

Sharing the Message

Speaking at spiritual centers, I was sharing a message with people who were already seekers. I knew I was not providing them new information. I knew that what I was saying had been said to them before, but I was listening to the call to share from my experience.

Sometimes it only takes one voice, one story, one moment for us to remember what we already know, and maybe my voice is helping the awakening and remembering. This book is the same. It does not offer anything your Higher Self does not already know. My intention is to remind you of your wholeness and your light, the way I was reminded when I finally opened my heart and chose myself and decided to live a healthy, happy life.

I began attending sacred circles, sound baths, and spiritual gatherings, stepping more fully into the spiritual community. I learned to receive. It was not only about me shining or helping everyone else. It was about accepting the love and light that others offered me and letting their wisdom nourish me, just as my desire is to nourish them.

I am grateful that the podcasts gave me a platform to share the Recover Your Soul process I had walked. The message of letting go of control, of turning attention inward, of learning to be OK when the people around you are not OK, reached more people than I expected.

My coaching work flourished, and I gained more clarity about the 9 Steps of Recover Your Soul. What began as a softer, more spiritual version of the 12 Steps evolved into a deep process of healing and awakening.

It incorporated teachings from spiritual masters, metaphysics, and energetic healing, all woven together into a path of recovering our souls, and it continues to evolve as I learn and grow.

We Are All Special, No One Is Special

One of the teachings that spoke to me in *A Course in Miracles* was that we are all special, and at the same time, no one is special. We are each unique, but no one is greater than another because we are one in the manifestation of God and the Universe.

This truth is essential in the journey of shining our light. Each of us longs to feel recognized, to know that our lives have significance. And we all deserve that. But true significance does not come from standing out, from saying, "Look at me, I am better than you." It comes from realizing our oneness, from coming together in awe of the truth.

That this way of being, this connection to a Higher Power of our own understanding, can truly heal our souls and change our lives. That we are not separate, but whole, and always have been.

Isn't that amazing?

I continue to be humbled by how far my voice has reached through the podcast. The emails, the messages, and the affirmations that my journey and my words have touched people and reminded them that they too can choose healing and happiness. It is both beautiful and deeply moving. I am profoundly grateful.

And yet, I remind myself daily that my number one responsibility is to stay in my own healing. My work is to remain in connection with Spirit and to shine light in my own life. If I begin to believe that I am doing it for my family, my friends, my podcast followers, or the world, I forget my soul's true purpose.

My purpose is to be awake and conscious. To take responsibility for my own happiness and well-being. When I live from that place, I can be fully present with others in my life, but without trying to carry responsibility for their choices or their healing. By tending my own light, I illuminate what is possible if they, too, decide to choose it.

And now, at the age of 55 as I write these words, I find myself filled with curiosity for the chapters still to come.

Stepping into Our Gifts

We need to stop living from worry and fear. We need to stop playing small. We need to stop trying to fix everything and everyone around us. Our number one responsibility is our own soul's experience. Being here, attending Earth School, and living this human life is incredibly important and valuable. Not a moment of it should be wasted.

Life is precious. We are each unique. We are each amazing. We hold gifts and talents that we often refuse to acknowledge, but it is time to step into them with humility, with courage, and with love. Remember: We are all special, and no one is special. We are all unique and beautiful, and each of us deserves to live healthy, joyful lives. And each of us gets to choose what that looks like. Within every person lies the possibility to create the life of his or her choosing.

Through Recover Your Soul coaching and the hundreds of people I've walked alongside, I have seen this truth come alive. Through the podcast, now reaching the top 1.5 percent of all podcasts globally, I've been honored to speak into the ears and hearts of so many.

But always the reminder returns: **Shining our light begins with staying connected and aware of our own daily experience.**

When we live from our most healed, authentic self, every interaction becomes an opportunity for healing. Relationships can shift in an instant when we show up in love.

I often think of *The Four Agreements* by Don Miguel Ruiz:
- Do not take things personally
- Do not make assumptions
- Always do your best
- Be impeccable with your word

Imagine if we truly lived by these simple yet profound agreements. Just these four can transform our perceptions and help us see through the eyes of love. To show up in every relationship as authentic, kind, compassionate, and clear would change the world. If humanity could stop taking everything personally, the shift into awakening would unfold even faster.

It's About the Journey

But we must begin with ourselves. We must begin with our own healing. Shining our light starts with looking honestly at our own experience. It does not mean every day will be easy. It does not mean we will avoid hardship or escape the ebb and flow of life. It certainly does not mean that everything will be perfect.

One of the greatest gifts I've received from this journey through years of journaling, through being present with my body and soul today, is the realization that there is no final destination. There are no wrong turns. There are only new experiences. It is not about arriving. It is about walking the path with awareness.

Life is complicated and sticky. There will be challenges and hurts. In recent years, I have walked through my mother's house burning down, both of my parents overcoming cancer, and now my father's partner is on her own cancer journey. I have watched my children go through difficulty and addiction as well as have successes and even bring a new soul into the world. I have pushed myself beyond what I thought I was capable of in every area of my life. **These are not easy paths. Yet even in these moments, something shifts when we show up trusting that everything is, in some way, working out for us.**

And sometimes it does not look the way we want. Sometimes people do not get well. Relationships often do not last, and the dreams we hold dearly may not come to pass. My lesson again and again is to let go. To remember that my transformation, though it has blessed my family, is not for them; it is for me and my own soul's awakening

Shining your light means accepting that some people may never heal in this lifetime. They may not choose joy. They may not get better. And still, our call is to love them in that choice. To release the need to control their experience and instead meet ourselves with compassion and tenderness in the grief of watching those we love walk difficult roads. To accept, allow, and love unconditionally through it all. **Because shining our light does not mean saving everyone; it means illuminating the path so that if others choose to walk it, they will see their Higher Self leading the way.**

The Recover Your Soul Process as a Way of Life

What I am most grateful for in what I call the Recover Your Soul™ 9-Step Process to Healing and Awakening is that it is not just a series of steps you take once. It is a lifelong path. It is a way of navigating the complexity of life with grace and compassion for ourselves and others, while always remembering our wholeness.

The Recover Your Soul Process shows us that our dissatisfaction and suffering are rooted in our perceptions, beliefs, patterns, and stories. Our pain comes from clinging to control and the illusion of power over external circumstances. When we acknowledge how unconscious beliefs have shaped our lives and behaviors, we gain the power to co-create with the Higher Power of our own understanding.

We learn to choose light and align with our authentic selves. We discover insights from old beliefs and patterns, and as we release them through compassion and forgiveness, we embrace new beliefs. We rewrite our stories to align with truth, with our gifts, and with the deeper strength within us. We begin to make conscious choices about how we engage with the world from our Higher Selves, supported by a regular spiritual practice that helps us shed old stories and live fully in the present moment.

And finally, we shine our light and live authentically, without control or judgment, embracing ourselves and the world as they are. That is the 9-Step Recover Your Soul Process. Each step is profound in itself, and together all the steps form a way of being that can meet all of life's challenges with love and compassion.

This process is about the soul and about remembering that we are energetic beings woven into an incredible web of consciousness that holds all of us. When we heal from this deeper spiritual place, we transform in ways the ego and mind cannot fully understand. We begin to release karmic repetitions of wounds and relationships that may go back further than this single lifetime. We soften ancestral patterns and generational traumas carried in our DNA and in the conditioning we received as children.

This powerful process of healing and awakening is not about reliving every wound or revisiting every shadow; it is about changing how we *see* it all. As our perception shifts, the suffering begins to release on an energetic level, quietly, profoundly, and often in ways that are beyond what words can describe.

I use this process every day as I walk in my still-sticky and complicated life, still with feelings, irritations, triggers, unmet expectations, disappointments, or fears. Sometimes it takes five minutes. Sometimes it takes days or weeks. But the moment something feels hard, I know: **This suffering is not because of what's happening outside me; it is because of a story or a belief inside me.**

That awareness alone brings me back to the way I choose to see it.

I remember: I am trying to control the uncontrollable. I am powerless over this situation. And so I turn inward with curiosity. What am I feeling beneath this reaction? What old pattern is being triggered? What part of me feels unsafe, unloved, or unseen?

I remind myself that I am not separate. I am connected to all that is, to Spirit, to Source. I am resourced in every moment. I can choose to see through the eyes of love instead of fear. And when the old voices rise, voices that say I am not enough, or that I must fix things, or that I must keep everyone happy, I touch those younger parts of myself with grace, compassion, and forgiveness. There are always more layers to be revealed, healed, and awakened.

And then I remember. I remember who I am. I remember my authentic, whole self. I connect with my Higher Self and with Spirit, and from that place I know I can face whatever is before me. I can have difficult conversations. I can take risks. I can even get it wrong and still be OK.

When I return to this truth, I step into life from my fully embodied self, walking with strength, compassion, and grace.

Living in the Present Moment

That is the process in its continuous circle. It is not only a way to heal the past, face long-term trauma, or update old belief systems. It is also a way to awaken — a way to raise consciousness, to step into the Higher Self, and to be fully present in this moment. It is the choice to let the pain of the past fall away and to hold onto what was beautiful and true.

I am actively rewriting the story of my life. The journals filled with pain are back on the shelf, not erased, not denied, but witnessed and loved. I don't need to keep wrapping myself in those blankets of suffering anymore. I can carry forward the truth, the love, and the connection that was always there beneath the chaos.

Rich supported our family for 30 years as a stone mason and builder, crafting beautiful yards, hardscapes, water features, and remodels. After decades of sustaining the business through talent, passion, and sometimes pure survival, he released it and stepped into a new chapter.

I believe he had used the incredible power of the Law of Attraction as he would share visions of what his next chapter would look like that allowed him to use his talents and also be part of a great team doing good in the world. And when an opportunity showed up 'out of the blue' for him to work for a local county in the open space division, he knew Spirit had answered his call.

He could put down the load that had begun to feel too heavy and step into this new chapter with an opportunity to be of service and continue to grow and learn more about himself.

And now, in this season, I see the vision I once wrote in Prosperity Plus coming alive, not because I forced it, but because life unfolded on its own terms. Bodhi, with his fire for board sports, carved out a life for himself by the ocean in California. He's a professional athlete, yes, but he's also out there creating art with his photography and video editing, living in a community that feeds his soul.

Alex, also in California, who walked through so much darkness in his younger years, has found a way to channel his love of art and design into real work and real meaning. With a partner who sees him, really sees him, and together they've built a life that now includes a baby boy, our grandson, Rocky. Watching him hold his newborn son is one of those moments that will be forever held as a shining moment of pure joy and love.

Do their lives look like the ones I used to try so hard to orchestrate when they were little? Not at all. And thank God. Their lives were never mine to design. Will their journeys be easy? Absolutely not, but I trust they will find the way. Their souls came through me for their own journeys, not so I could direct every chapter. That's been one of the hardest lessons and one of the deepest gifts in recovering my soul is letting go of my children.

They're not "fixed." They still have their struggles, their own healing work, and their own relationship with addiction. But they're standing in lives they chose. And for now, there's light where there used to be so much dark. That's enough. The present moment is enough.

We are more connected as a family than we ever were in the years when I was clinging so tightly. And it's not because I solved everything. It's because I finally let go. That control still tries to creep in; it's sneaky. But the difference now is that I can see it, breathe, and come back to presence instead of falling into the old traps.

I release the future, too, and the worry, the obsession with fixing everything, and the pressure to hold the whole world together. I trust that life is unfolding. When I stay here, right now, I see that even the messy, complicated feelings are part of presence. And in that presence, I can trust. I can co-create. I can walk forward knowing that the more authentic I am in this moment, the more beautifully life unfolds. **Life is not happening to me. Life is happening with me.**

So I keep returning to the practices that ground me. I let myself change, grow, stretch, love, and shine a little brighter every single day. And I give myself permission to be exactly who I am in each moment: raw, imperfect, real.

To be in the world, but not of the world. To walk in wholeness, to live in love, and to shine my light.

Your Path Awaits

I am walking this path, and you can too. Your stories, just like mine, carry incredible richness and value. You have known deep pain, and you have known incredible joy. You have walked through tragedy and trauma, and you have also experienced success, adventure, and love. Within each of these stories lies wisdom and guidance about your soul's purpose and the lessons your soul came here to learn.

If you are ready to release the pain story, as Eckhart Tolle calls it, the "pain body," and to step more fully into your authentic self, there is a way forward. It might be the Recover Your Soul path, or it might be another path entirely. **What matters is not the name of the path but your decision to walk it.**

The call is to begin a spiritual journey that leads you back to your wholeness and your Higher Self.

There is nothing wrong with you. You are not broken. You are already whole. And you too can remember the fullness of who you are and live from your authentic self.

You can let go of trying to control everyone and everything around you. It is safe to let go. You can choose to see through the eyes of love. Even if you do not yet know how to walk the path, trust this: your soul remembers the way.

Working the Steps in Your Own Life

Recover Your Soul - STEP 9

9. Shine Your Light
Live Authentically: **Let go of control and judgment, embodying your True Self and allowing life to unfold with grace and acceptance.**
Be a Beacon of Love: **Allow your presence and peace to inspire others, becoming a light for awakening and transformation in the world.**

***

I didn't set out to create a process. I set out to save my own life. What became the Recover Your Soul Process grew out of my journals, my tears, my sobriety, my failures, and those quiet, powerful whispers from Spirit that said, "Rachel, *Recover Your Soul.*"

The Recover Your Soul Process is not a quick fix, a checklist, or something you do once and then set aside. It is a lifelong path. It is a way of walking through the complexity of life with awareness, love, and compassion for yourself first, and then for everyone around you.

You have walked with me through these 9 Steps, each one an invitation to remember what has always been true: you are whole. You are not broken. You are not behind. You are not too much, and you are not here to settle and play small. You are a soul on a journey of awakening, and everything you have lived, including your pain, joy, mistakes, and victories, is part of your sacred unfolding.

The steps of Recover Your Soul remind us to release control, to see through the eyes of love, to rewrite our stories, to step into our Higher Selves, and to shine our light. They are not about perfection or escape but about being fully conscious in your life. They bring us back again and again to this precious moment, the only place where healing and wholeness are found.

And so the invitation is simple: Keep walking. Keep choosing love over fear. Continue to show up with authenticity and compassion. Keep trusting that your soul knows the way with a soft whisper of knowing your truth. **I am whole. I am light. I shine my light into the world.**

I'm grateful I don't walk this alone. Mattie, my friend and collaborator on this book, has been shoulder-to-shoulder with me, working these steps in her own life and helping me share this message with you. We are living proof that this process offers profound transformation. It changes families. It softens relationships. It gives us back our own hearts.

If you'd like to keep walking this path with me, I invite you to listen to these episodes from the *Recover Your Soul* podcast, where I share more stories, practices, and conversations to support your awakening. Together, we remember, we heal, and we shine brighter as souls who know who we truly are.

Podcasts on Shining Your Light

https://recoveryoursoulbook.com/

The Invitation to Recover Your Soul

There is a voice calling to you right now, just as it called to me in that car ride home from Thailand. It may be quiet, barely a whisper beneath the noise of your daily life. Or it may be loud, impossible to ignore, demanding that you finally listen. However it comes to you, it is the voice of your soul and your Higher Self calling you home to who you really are. **"Recover Your Soul."**

These three words changed everything for me. They can change everything for you, too.

Recovering my soul has been a journey of self-love and compassion as I slowly recovered all the parts of me, the light and the shadow, and allowed them to share the gifts they had for me. During those years when I felt lost in the storm of pain and overwhelm, I couldn't see that my Higher Self, my Spirit guides, and my Higher Power were with me all along. They nudged me and soothed me the best they could, but it was not until I was ready, until I finally reached my breaking point where I let go of control and asked with an open and receptive heart, that the path to recovering my soul was made clear to me.

This Is Your Story, Too

The story I have shared with you is not only mine. It belongs to all of us. The details may differ, but the journey is universal because it is ours, a hero's journey of the soul. We all come to places where we feel lost. We all discover moments when the life we are living does not align with the life our soul came here to live. **And we all reach a point when the pain of staying the same becomes greater than the fear of change.**

You may be in the depths of your own dark night of the soul right now. You may be numbing yourself with substances, distractions, or endless busyness. You may be trying to control everyone around you, hoping the external world will finally soothe your inner needs. You may be shape-shifting and people-pleasing your way through life, trying to be what you think others expect of you.

Codependency and people-pleasing are not faults or defects. They are protections and come from a place of wanting to love and be loved. As I have discovered the process I call recovering your soul, I have found a place for all the parts of me that I have recovered and brought home to the inner sanctuary of my heart. I kept my heart closed even to those I loved the most, but I have now discovered that it has enough space to hold everything. I continue to discover more and more about myself and find it fascinating how deep and complicated we all are in our messy beauty.

Wherever you are on this journey, please hear this:

> *You are exactly where you need to be.*
> *Your pain has purpose.*
> *Your struggles have meaning.*
> *Your story, whatever it looks like, is sacred.*

Earth School and Divine Remembering

We are all souls having a human experience in what I have come to understand as Earth School. We did not come here to be perfect. We came here to learn, grow, and remember who we truly are through the very process of forgetting and finding ourselves again.

Your soul chose this life, these circumstances, and these challenges, not as punishment, but as the exact curriculum needed for your evolution. Every difficult person in your life is a teacher. Every painful experience is a lesson. Every moment of suffering is an invitation to remember your divinity.

The past has changed for me. It is no longer a pain story but one of transformation and healing. I can still touch those difficult moments, as I did writing and speaking the stories included in this book, and can feel the feelings of sadness, disappointment, regret, heartbreak, disconnection, insecurity, and hopelessness.

But they wash over me like waves, and I feel a knowing that these feelings are valuable and important. I can rise above them, the transformed butterfly, and see them with new perception and compassion for the self I was in each of those moments, who was doing the best she could. I honor her experiences. From this elevated place, I can see that the pain had purpose, and although I can wish the path had not been so difficult, I am grateful that it has brought me to exactly where I am today.

This does not mean we are asked to be passive about pain or to accept abuse. It means we are invited to see our experiences, all of them, through the eyes of love rather than through the eyes of victimhood. It means we can remember that we are not broken beings in need of fixing, but divine beings who sometimes forget our true nature. **Recovering your soul is the process of remembering your wholeness.**

The 9 Steps: A Way of Living

The Recover Your Soul™ Process to Healing and Awakening steps are a framework for living, a way of perceiving reality, and a set of principles to return to again and again as you navigate the complexities of being human.

You will likely go through these steps numerous times in your life. Each cycle will take you deeper. Each journey will reveal new layers of healing, new opportunities for growth, and new invitations to shine your light even brighter.

My understanding and spiritual journey continue to expand and transform. So much is healing and changing within me that I feel I am not even the same as I was a month or year ago, as more is always being revealed.

Working on this book brought up all of my deepest wounds and feelings of unworthiness and self-doubt that were still lying dormant in the depths of my shadow self. While I sat in the deep pain and discomfort of those limiting and unkind beliefs, I knew they were being revealed to be healed.

On some days, you may find yourself back at Step 1, facing suffering that you thought was already resolved. This is not failure. It is the spiral-based nature of growth. We do not heal in straight lines; we heal in spirals, circling back to familiar places but from higher ground, with more wisdom, greater compassion, and deeper understanding.

This is the dance of the Recover Your Soul path. This is the rhythm of awakening. This is what it means to live as both human and divine.

Seeing through the Eyes of Love

The ultimate goal of recovering your soul is not to eliminate pain from your life; rather, it is to transform your relationship with pain and suffering. It is to develop the ability to see through the eyes of love instead of the eyes of fear, to perceive with the vision of your Higher Self instead of the limited perspective of your wounded ego.

When you see through a new perception, you understand that everyone is doing the best they can with the tools at their disposal. You begin to see that hurt people hurt people, and healed people heal people. You realize that the one who triggered your deepest wounds was most likely acting from their own unhealed pain.

This shift does not mean you abandon boundaries. It does not mean you accept mistreatment. It means learning how to hold truth and compassion simultaneously. You can protect yourself and still recognize the divine spark in others. **You can say no with loving detachment. You can walk away carrying forgiveness instead of resentment.**

My Woo-Woo Bubble and Choosing Love

I believe it is no mistake that at this very important time in the history of humanity, I am also one of those who are choosing awakening. There have been many reminders and messages along the way that I am here on purpose and it is safe to shine my light.

This includes the story my parents tell that they did not plan to have children until they were looking out at the stars on a clear night in New Mexico and both heard a call that a soul was to come.

My father recently shared a story of Ram Dass carrying me around as a baby in Santa Fe as part of my wild hippy upbringing. I did not know this as I listened to hours and hours of his talks on consciousness and awakening as part of my spiritual path. However, when my father shared this precious story, I knew there was a larger reason why Ram Dass's words had spoken to me so deeply.

I have begun to trust the guidance that is leading me farther out into what I call the woo-woo and the science of quantum and energy. It can feel a bit like I live in a bubble that doesn't always align with the world where I buy my groceries or eat out with friends. But at the same time, I know that I am choosing each moment, and I am choosing love.

If I question whether the bubble is real, I come back to the idea that it doesn't matter. This decision to live from a spiritual path has given me a happy and healthy life and I will choose this over the fear and worry and control that only made me miserable for more than 20 years. I choose love.

The Invitation

Right now, in this very moment, you have a choice. You can close this book and return to the familiar patterns of your life, hoping that things will improve on their own. Or you can listen to the voice calling to you, perhaps louder now than when you started reading, and step onto the path to Recover Your Soul.

This is not an easy path. I cannot promise you that it will be comfortable, convenient, or quick. Recovery of any kind requires courage, commitment, and a willingness to face truths you may have been avoiding. Recover Your Soul invites you to explore your deepest wounds, examine your most cherished beliefs, and release attachments to ways of being that may have served you in the past but now hold you back.

But I will promise you this: it is worth it. Every uncomfortable conversation with yourself. Every moment of sitting with complicated feelings instead of numbing them. Every choice to respond from love instead of reacting from fear. Every step toward authenticity and away from performance. It is all worth it.

Our life, our precious incarnation in this body as who we are for this lifetime, is so important and so special.

It is not about denying what is hard or spiritually bypassing the process. It is about fully embodying our life and choosing the way we see it. It is about feeling even more deeply and allowing those feelings to show us what we need and want to learn from the experiences. It is about connecting even more deeply to the God of your understanding and cultivating a relationship with that energy that aligns with your soul and Higher Self.

Because on the other side of this work, not at the end because there is no end, but woven throughout the journey, is a life of unprecedented freedom. Freedom from the need to control outcomes. Freedom from the exhausting work of managing other people's emotions. Freedom from the constant anxiety of trying to be someone you are not. **You will discover that you are enough, exactly as you are. You will learn that you do not need anyone else's validation to feel valuable. You will realize that your worth is not determined by your productivity, appearance, achievements, or ability to make others happy.**

Starting Where You Are

You do not need to wait until you have more time, more money, more support, or more clarity to begin. You do not need to figure out all 9 Steps before you take the first one. You do not need to be perfect, ready, or sure about anything except your willingness and a decision to try something different. **The Recover Your Soul Process begins with a single moment of honest recognition:**

This is not working. Then: I need something different. Followed by: I am willing to change.

From that moment of willingness, everything becomes possible. Not immediately. Not easily. But inevitably. The path will appear as you walk it. The teachers will arrive when you are ready for the lessons. The community will gather when you need support.

There is a movement of consciousness that is growing, and I am honored and humbled to be a voice that is offering hope and healing to so many. I am not special or have any gifts that are not available to all of us because we are all special and have gifts. I am just learning to trust and open to the flow of guidance that speaks to and through me.

I continue to focus on my own healing and awakening as my first priority, and then with humility offer it to those who can remember their own wholeness through the stories and language I use.

The Voice That Called to Me Calls to You

In that airplane over the Pacific Ocean in 2018, after my last drinks, after three weeks of remembering who I was beneath all the pain, addiction, and control, I heard a voice as clear as my own speak to me: **"It is time to heal."**

And later I was given the directive: "Recover your soul."

That same voice is calling to you now. It may use different words, but the message is the same: Come home to yourself. Remember who you are. You are not broken. You are not beyond hope. You are not too lost to be found.

We are not broken. There is nothing wrong with us. We are enough, and we are remembering our wholeness. Your stories are your strength and your journey, and when you decide you are ready, your soul will lead the way.

Your soul is calling you home. Not to a physical place, but to the truth of who you are. To the love that you are. To the light that you are.

The journey of recovering your soul is, in essence, a journey of remembering. Remembering that beneath every addiction is a spiritual longing. Beneath every compulsive behavior is a soul seeking connection. Beneath every attempt to control lies a heart that wants to feel safe.

You are that soul. You are that longing. You are that heart.

And you are calling yourself home.

Listen to that voice. Trust that whisper. Take the first step.

All you need to do is listen to that voice calling to you, the voice of your own soul, and whisper back, "Yes. I am ready to recover my soul."

With all my love,

Rev. Rachel

Book Resources

Linktree https://linktr.ee/RecoverYourSoul

https://www.instagram.com/recoveryoursoulpodcast/

https://www.youtube.com/@RecoverYourSoul

https://insighttimer.com/recoveryoursoul

https://www.facebook.com/recoveryoursoul.net/

https://www.recoveryoursoul.net/